EVIDENCE OF ALIEN CONTACT

Ken Hudnall
Omega Press
El Paso, TX 79912

EVIDENCE OF ALIEN CONTACT
COPYRIGHT © 2014 KEN HUDNALL

All rights reserved. No part of this book may be reproduced or transmitted in any form or by any means, graphic, electronic, or mechanical, including photocopying, recording, taping or by any information storage or retrieval system, without the permission in writing from the publisher.

OMEGA PRESS

An imprint of Omega Communications Group, Inc.

For information contact:

Omega Press

5823 N. Mesa, #839

El Paso, Texas 79912

Or http://www.kenhudnall.com

FIRST EDITION

Printed in the United States of America

OTHER WORKS BY THE SAME AUTHOR UNDER THE NAME KEN HUDNALL FROM OMEGA PRESS

MANHATTAN CONSPIRACY SERIES
Blood on the Apple
Capitol Crimes
Angel of Death

THE OCCULT CONNECTION
UFOs, Secret Societies and Ancient Gods
The Hidden Race
Flying Saucers
UFOs and the Supernatural
UFOs and Secret Societies
UFOs and Ancient Gods

DARKNESS
When Darkness Falls
Fear The Darkness

SPIRITS OF THE BORDER
(with Connie Wang)
The History and Mystery of El Paso Del Norte
The History and Mystery of Fort Bliss, Texas

(with Sharon Hudnall)
The History and Mystery of the Rio Grande
The history and Mystery of New Mexico
The History and Mystery of the Lone Star State
The History and Mystery of Arizona
The History and Mystery of Tombstone, AZ
The History and Mystery of Colorado
Echoes of the Past
El Paso: A City of Secrets
Tales From The Nightshift
The History and Mystery of Sin City

The History and Mystery of Concordia

THE ESTATE SALE MURDERS
Dead Man's Diary

Northwood Conspiracy

No Safe Haven; Homeland Insecurity

Where No Car Has Gone Before

Seventy Years and No Losses: The History of the Sun Bowl

How Not To Get Published

PUBLISHED BY PAJA BOOKS
The Occult Connection: Unidentified Flying Objects

DEDICATION

As with all of my books, I could not have completed this book if not for my lovely wife, Sharon.

Table of Contents

WHO CAME FIRST? 9
THE ANNUNAKI, THE WATCHERS AND THE IGIGI 15
DIRECT SIGNS OF ALIEN INTERVENTION . 27
UFOS IN RELIGION 47
EVIDENCE OF EARLY ADVANCED CIVILIZATIONS 61
ABDUCTIONS AND VISITATIONS 79
BY ALIENS 79
ANOMOLOUS CITIES AND TECHNOLOGY .. 91
SIGNS OF LIFE ON THE MOON 101
ARE ALIENS ON THE MOON? 121
UNDERGROUND ALIEN BASES AROUND THE WORLD 131
UNDERGROUND BASES IN THE UNITED STATES 145
INDEX 223

CHAPTER ONE
WHO CAME FIRST?

As we wrote in UFOs and Ancient Gods[1], there are numerous legends of ancient gods interacting with early man to create civilization and all of its wonders. Of course, there are as many who believe that the ancient gods were just myths and make believe. Others believe that these ancient gods

Figure 1: Atlas

---

[1] Hudnall, Ken, UFOs and Ancient Gods, Omega Press, El Paso, Texas 79912 (2014)

were actually aliens who came to this planet to exploit it for its natural resources. The question is did the gods create mankind or did the gods come to exploit a pre-existing mankind?

FALLEN ANGELS

We all know the story in the Christian Bible of when God cast out 1/3 of his angels from heaven to earth because they had joined Lucifer in a rebellion against God. These fallen angels were called the Nephilim in the Bible and interbred with human females, which shows that the "gods" and humans were related.

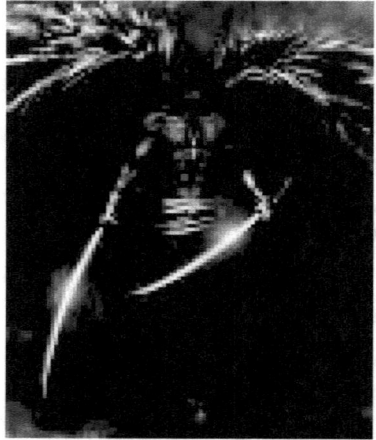

Figure 2: Fallen Angels

If as Zacharia Sitchin was correct and the Annunaki were space travelers who came to earth to exploit it for its riches, the so called fallen angels were rebellious space men who decided to take advantage of the locals. This would not be the first time that primitives mistook advanced beings and technology as something coming from the gods. Prime examples of this concept were the Cargo Cults found in the Pacific during and after World War II. The primitive tribesmen of the area found crashed cargo planes and viewed what was on them as riches sent by the gods. A religion grew up around the idea that such riches came from the gods and praying to them would keep the flow of goods coming.

In their rights, the Sumerians claimed that gods came from the heavens above and taught them many works and wonders of life. The chief teacher for the Sumerians was called Oannes and was said to be half fish and half man. The Sumerians accurately recorded and described our galaxy and every planet within it down to the colors, textures, rotations, and locations of them. How would they know all of this information about other planets?

The Sumerians claim that Gods from above, "the enlightened ones," came down from the "heavens" and taught them many arts. This sounds very much like God's fallen angels may have come to earth and taught many secrets to mankind and portrayed themselves as Gods in their own right. These Gods would come and go as they please into and out of our planet. Or perhaps, these superior beings were space travelers? Actually, these being have many things in common with our modern day aliens. Think about all the ancient Gods recorded through-out our history. Could all those civilizations who claimed to know and walk with

Figure 3: St. Michael leading the hosts of Heaven

these Gods just be plain crazy or perhaps there is truth in what they said?

Another theory, which has a lot to be said for it is that current civilization was based on a much older advanced civilization that was destroyed by some cataclysm. The "gods" who roamed the planet and taught early man may well have been survivors of this early civilization and imparted their secrets to early man. This would account for the stories of early man walking and talking with the "gods".

Of course there are also stories that the gods of earth were survivors of a war in the heavens. But not all are familiar with the war that broke out in heaven, when it was said that Jesus cleansed the heavens of Satan and his demons and casted them down to the earth. The Christian Bible's Book of Revelation describes a "war in heaven" between angels led by the Archangel Michael versus those led by "the dragon", identified with "the devil and Satan", which were defeated and thrown down to the earth. Could this planet have been used as a prison for these defeated warriors?

Revelation's "war in heaven" has been compared to the idea of fallen angels and possible parallels have been proposed in the Hebrew Bible and Dead Sea Scrolls. The Bible says that Satan keeps transforming himself into an angel of light and many people claim to have seen angels of light today as well. Those who favor this theory believe that the idea of Aliens actually comes from Satan. These same fanatics say that anything that is not found in Almighty God's word comes from Satan, as a result of this narrow minded attitude the truth is hidden from sight.

Under this theory, every time someone was "supposedly" being abducted by aliens, and they prayed to the Lord to protect them, it was said that the aliens would disappear. If you ever watch these "alien abductions" shows, you'll see the same thing. The few people who cried out to the Lord are said to have found that the abduction stopped. How much of this was real and how much was an attempt on the part of the entities to support the idea of religious intervention? From a practical standpoint, religion is a fantastic control mechanism as anything taboo as contrary to the religion of the time is safe from discovery by the vast majority of the population.

Scientists who do their research from their own private ivory towers believe that abductees suffer from sleep paralysis and they are imagining that they are being attacked at night. These victims of so called alien abduction see all kinds of things from aliens to old hags, a mysterious dark man and others of the same ilk. Some of those who believe that they are actually abducted report being held down not being able to speak.

The origin of demons is not commonly known in our time. However, in ancient times it was well understood that demons are the disembodied spirits of the Nephilim. The reader will recall that the Nephilim (the earth-born giants of the days of Noah) were the offspring of what were described as fallen angels and the 'daughters of men.' According to numerous ancient rabbinic and Early Church texts, when the Nephilim died their spirits became disembodied and roamed the earth, harassing mankind.

Mysterious teachers, strange aerial craft and other things we would call UFO events have been with us for thousands of years, however, there are many who choose to place the beginning of the modern UFO phenomenon at the point of pilot Kenneth Arnold's sighting in 1947 (which many prefer to do), there is nevertheless a direct relationship between UFOs and the fallen angels, and stories of encounters with angels handed down through the scriptures of many religions, and some of the arguments in favor of the angelic interpretation of ancient and modern UFO accounts. It interesting that most people regard angels as existing in a spiritual plane only. Angels (fallen or not) exist in both the physical and spiritual planes.

Figure 4: There are many stories about UFOs in ancient Egypt.

According to the Bible, so rife were the Nephilim and their own offspring, along with Satan's offspring which had polluted the gene pool of man eons earlier, that only Noah was pure in his ancestry and so God sent the flood. Now, the fallen angels are once again loose on the Earth, and once again mixing their DNA with ours.

CHAPTER TWO
THE ANNUNAKI, THE WATCHERS AND THE IGIGI

Figure 5: An Annunaki as describ3ed by ancient records

The Anunnaki[2] (also transcribed as: Annunaki, Anunna, Anunnaku, Ananaki and other variations) are a group of deities in ancient Mesopotamian cultures (i.e. Sumerian, Akkadian, Assyrian, and Babylonian). The name is variously written "da-nuna", "da-nuna-ke4-ne", or "da-nun-na", meaning something to the effect of "those of royal blood" or "princely offspring". According to The Oxford Companion to World Mythology, the Anunnaki "are the Sumerian deities of the old primordial line; they are chthonic deities of fertility,

---

[2] See the work of Zacharia Sitchin entitled "The Earth Chronicles".

associated eventually with the underworld, where they became judges. They take their name from the old sky god An[3] (Anu).

Their relation to the group of gods known as the Igigi[4] is unclear – at times the names are used synonymously but in the Atra-Hasis flood myth the Igigi are the sixth generation of the Gods who have to work for the Anunnaki, rebelling after 40 days and replaced by the creation of humans.

Jeremy Black and Anthony Green[5] offer a slightly different perspective on the Igigi and the Anunnaki, writing that "Igigu or Igigi is a term introduced in the Old Babylonian Period as a name for the (ten) "great gods". While it sometimes kept that sense in later periods, from Middle Assyrian and Babylonian times on it is generally used to refer to the gods of heaven collectively, just as the term Anunnakku (Anuna) was later used to refer to the gods of the underworld. In the Epic of Creation it is said that there are 300 Igigu in heaven."

The Anunnaki appear in the Babylonian creation myth, Enuma Elish. In the late version magnifying Marduk, after the creation of mankind, Marduk divides the Anunnaki and assigns them to their proper stations, three hundred in heaven, three hundred on the earth. In gratitude, the Anunnaki, the "Great Gods", built Esagila, the splendid: "They raised high the head of Esagila equaling Apsu. Having built a stage-tower as high as Apsu, they set up in it

---

[3] The original King of the Gods
[4] According to Sitchin, the Igigi are those referred to as the Watchers.
[5] Black, Jeremy and Green, Anthony: <u>Gods, Demons and Symbols of Ancient Mesopotamia: An Illustrated Dictionary</u> University of Texas Press (Aug 1992)

an abode for Marduk, Enlil, and Ea." Then they built their own shrines.

The Annunaki are mentioned in The Epic of Gilgamesh when Utnapishtim tells the story of the flood. The seven judges of hell are called the Annunaki, and they set the land aflame as the storm is approaching. Clearly the Annunaki were looked at as extremely powerful.

According to later Assyrian and Babylonian myth, the Anunnaki were the children of Anu and Ki, brother and sister gods, themselves the children of Anshar and Kishar (Skypivot and Earthpivot, the Celestial poles), who in turn were the children of Lahamu and Lahmu ("the muddy ones"), names given to the gatekeepers of the Abzu (House of Far Waters) temple at Eridu, the site at which the creation was thought to have occurred. Finally, Lahamu and Lahmu were the children of Tiamat (Goddess of the Ocean) and Abzu (God of Fresh Water).

There are also stories in the various religious works about the watchers. Watcher is a term used in connection with biblical angels. Watcher occurs in both plural and singular forms in the Book of Daniel (2nd century BC), where reference is made to their holiness. The apocryphal Books of Enoch (1st and 2nd centuries BC) refer to both good and bad Watchers, with a primary focus on the rebellious ones. These watchers were said to be assigned to watch the earth and keep track of what the humans were up to. Others say that the Watchers may well be the Igigi, assigned to stay on board the base craft of the Annunaki expedition. Interestingly enough when man first went into space an unknown orbiting craft was found in a polar orbit.

It was named the Black Knight and is rarely spoken of by those in authority.

There is a great deal of information to be found about the Watchers in the Book of Enoch, an early religious tract about a man named Enoch and his travels and travails. There were actually two books called the Book of Enoch[6].

In the Book of Enoch[7], the Watchers are referred to as angels dispatched to Earth to watch over the humans. They soon begin to lust for human women and, at the prodding of their leader Samyaza, defect en masse to illicitly instruct humanity and procreate among them. The offspring of these unions are the Nephilim, savage giants who pillage the earth and endanger humanity. Samyaza and his associates further taught their human charges arts and technologies such as weaponry, cosmetics, mirrors, sorcery, and other techniques that would otherwise be discovered gradually over time by humans, not foisted upon them all at once. Eventually God allows a Great Flood to rid the earth of the Nephilim, but first sends Uriel to warn Noah so as not to eradicate the human race. The Watchers are bound "in the valleys of the Earth" until Judgment Day. (Jude verse 6 says that these fallen angels are kept "in everlasting chains under darkness" until Judgment Day.)

The chiefs of tens of these fallen angels also listed in the Book of Enoch are as follows:

And these are the names of their leaders: Sêmîazâz, their leader, Arâkîba, Râmêêl, Kôkabîêl, Tâmîêl, Râmîêl,

---

[6] The Book of Enoch, Oxford: Clarendon, 1893, reprinted in 1895. Republished by Boston, MA: Samuel Weiser; 2003. ISBN 1-57863-259-5

[7] The Book of Enoch or 1 Enoch: Translated from the Editor's Ethiopic Text, Oxford: Clarendon, 1912.

Dânêl, Êzêqêêl, Barâqîjâl, Asâel, Armârôs, Batârêl, Anânêl, Zaqîêl, Samsâpêêl, Satarêl, Tûrêl, Jômjâêl, and Sariêl[8].

The book of Enoch also lists leaders of the 200 fallen angels who married and commenced in unnatural union with human women, and who taught forbidden knowledge. Some are also listed in Book of Raziel (Sefer Raziel HaMalakh), the Zohar and Jubilees.

- Araqiel (also Arakiel, Araqael, Araciel, Arqael, Sarquael, Arkiel, and Arkas) taught humans the signs of the earth. However, in the Sibylline Oracles, Araqiel is referred to not as a fallen angel, or Watcher, but as one of the 5 angels who lead the souls of men to judgment, the other 4 being Ramiel, Uriel, Samiel, and Azazel.
- Armaros (also Amaros) in Enoch I taught men the resolving of enchantments.
- Azazel taught men to make knives, swords, shields, and how to devise ornaments and cosmetics.
- Gadreel taught the art of cosmetics, the use of weapons and killing blows. It was he who led Eve astray in the Garden of Eden.
- Baraqel (Baraqiel) taught men astrology
- Bezaliel mentioned in Enoch I, left out of most translations because of damaged manuscripts and problematic transmission of the text.
- Chazaqiel (sometimes Ezeqeel or Cambriel) taught men the signs of the clouds (meteorology).

---

[8] R. H. Charles translation, The Book of the Watchers, Chapter VI.

- Kokabiel (also Kakabel, Kochbiel, Kokbiel, Kabaiel, and Kochab), In the Book of Raziel he is a high-ranking, holy angel. In Enoch I, he is a fallen Watcher, resident of the nether realms, and commands 365,000 surrogate spirits to do his bidding. Among other duties, he instructs his fellows in astrology.
- Penemue "taught mankind the art of writing with ink and paper," and taught "the children of men the bitter and the sweet and the secrets of wisdom." (I Enoch 69.8)
- Sariel (also Suriel) taught mankind about the courses of the moon (at one time regarded as forbidden knowledge).
- Samyaza (also Shemyazaz, Shamazya, Semiaza, Shemhazi, Semyaza and Amezyarak) is one of the leaders of the fall from heaven in Vocabulaire de l' Angelologie.
- Shamsiel, once a guardian of Eden as stated in the Zohar, served as one of the two chief aides to the archangel Uriel (the other aide being Hasdiel) when Uriel bore his standard into battle, and is the head of 365 legions of angels and also crowns prayers, accompanying them to the 5th heaven. In Jubilees, he is referred to as one of the Watchers. He is a fallen angel who teaches the signs of the sun.
- Yeqon (also Jeqon or Yaqum, "he shall rise") was the ringleader who first tempted the other Watchers into having sexual relations with humans. His accomplices were Asbeel, Gadreel, Penemue, and

Kasdaye (or Kasadya). Together, they were known as the Five Satans.

The account of the Book of Enoch has been associated with the passage in Genesis 6:1-4, which speaks of Sons of God instead of Watchers:

> *When men began to multiply on earth and daughters were born to them, the sons of God saw how beautiful the daughters of man were, and so they took for their wives as many of them as they chose. Then the Lord said: "My spirit shall not remain in man forever, since he is but flesh. His days shall comprise one hundred and twenty years." At that time the Nephilim appeared on earth (as well as later), after the sons of God had intercourse with the daughters of man, who bore them sons. They were the heroes of old, the men of renown.*
> —Genesis 6:1-4

Second Book of Enoch

For the masculine given name, see Grigori (given name) and Grigory

The Jewish pseudepigraphon Second Book of Enoch (Slavonic Enoch) refers to the Grigori, who are the same as the Watchers of 1 Enoch. The Slavic word Grigori used in the book is a transcription of a Greek word in post-classical times, meaning "wakeful".

Chapter 18 presents the Grigori as countless soldiers of human appearance, "their size being greater than that of great giants[9]". They are located in the fifth heaven and identified as "the Grigori, who with their prince Satanail rejected the Lord of light". One version of 2 Enoch adds that their number was 200 myriads. Furthermore, some "went down on to earth from the Lord's throne" and there married women and "befouled the earth with their deeds", resulting in confinement under earth. The number of those who descended to earth is generally put at three, but Andrei A. Orlov, while quoting the text as saying three, remarks in a footnote that some manuscripts put them at 200 or even 200 myriads.

Chapter 29, referring to the second day of creation, before the creation of human beings, says that "one from out the order of angels" or, according to other versions of 2 Enoch, "one of the order of archangels" or "one of the ranks of the archangels conceived an impossible thought, to place his throne higher than the clouds above the earth, that he might become equal in rank to [the Lord's] power. And [the Lord] threw him out from the height with his angels, and he was flying in the air continuously above the bottomless." Although in this chapter the name "Satanail" is mentioned only in a heading added in one manuscript, this chapter is often understood to refer to Satanail and his angels, the Grigori.

The Mercer Dictionary of the Bible makes a distinction between the Grigori and the fallen angels by stating that in fifth heaven, Enoch sees "the giants whose brothers were the fallen angels." The longer recension of 2

---

[9] This could be the basis for the race of giants discovered in North America – See U.F.O.s and Ancient Gods, by Ken Hudnall.

Enoch 18:3 identifies the prisoners of second heaven as the angels of Satanail.

Much of what we known about the Annunaki came from the research of Zacharia Sitchin. He has long been the major investigator of the Sumerian records dating from the earliest days of Sumerian civilization. Zechariah Sitchin[10] believes that his work shows that many of the Biblical Stories of gods and angels originated from Sumeria and the activities of the Annunaki.

Further, he claims that the Annunaki were on Earth about 450,000 years ago, primarily looking for gold which was very important in their culture, and perhaps for their longevity. This gold prospecting was said to have originally taken place in Africa and as we shall see there is much evidence to support this premise.

Not surprisingly, such advanced beings in ships and with 'magical' technology were viewed as gods by the primitive humans. The main person was Anu who was in charge overall and probably remained in his ship in orbit around Earth.

Beneath him were Ninhursag, Enlil (brother and sister) and Enki, as well as Marduk, Inanna and a variety of minor deities each with their own areas of responsibility.

---

[10] Zecharia Sitchin (July 11, 1920 – October 9, 2010) was an Azerbaijani-born American author of books proposing an explanation for human origins involving ancient astronauts. Sitchin attributes the creation of the ancient Sumerian culture to the Anunnaki, which he states was a race of extraterrestrials from a planet beyond Neptune called Nibiru. He believed this hypothetical planet of Nibiru to be in an elongated, elliptical orbit in the Earth's own Solar System, asserting that Sumerian mythology reflects this view. Sitchin's books have sold millions of copies worldwide and have been translated into more than 25 languages.

From careful reading of the clay tablets and interpretation of the carvings on the cylinder seals found in ancient Sumer, Sitchin has pieced together a detailed history of the Annunaki which he believed showed that our history was not the true history of this planet.

The full story is very long and worth reading if you

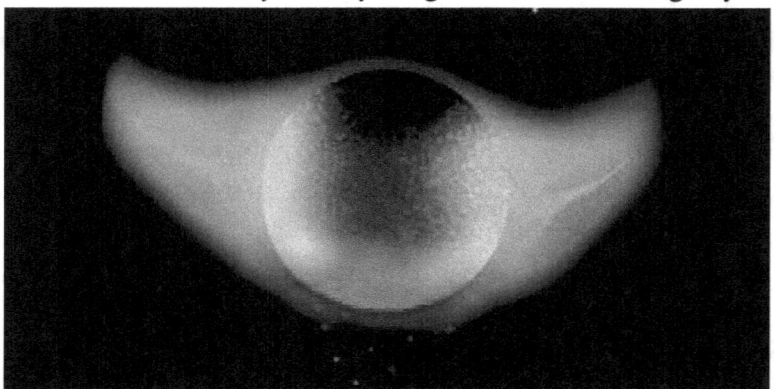

Figure 6: Planet X or Nibiru

are at all interested in this aspect of alien intervention in human affairs. There are six books in his series titled 'The Earth Chronicles'. In them, he takes the story of the Annunaki from their origin on another planet (which has since been known as Nibiru, Planet X, Marduk and The Twelfth Planet), and tells of how they mined gold, manipulated the genes of humanity and generally altered the normal run of affairs on Earth.

For example, there is a puzzling passage in Genesis chapter 6 verse 4 which reads; *"There were giants in the earth in those days; and also after that, when the sons of God came in unto the daughters of men, and they; bare children unto them, the same became mighty men which were of old, men of renown."*

A different version has that same passage as, "*The Nephilim were upon the Earth in those days and thereafter too. Those sons of the gods who cohabited with the daughters of the Adam, and they bore children into them. They were the Mighty Ones of Eternity, the People of the Shem.*"

This could be explained as the Annunaki coming down from above and co-habiting with human women. Instead of giants, the term 'Fallen Ones' is better explained by their descent from the heavens in their ships. The Nephilim were, according to Sitchin, the Annunaki.

All this is, of course, interesting. But the main interest to me is the influence these aliens have had upon us.

Look at the civilization of Sumer as a start. This advanced culture seemingly sprang up overnight from a gaggle of simple primitives. This new civilization bore the hallmarks of an aware and technologically capable society at a time when no-one can point to any possible precursor. Taxes, irrigation, public buildings, a powerful priesthood, a civil code, factories, all of these trapping of a complex society just appeared pretty much out of nowhere. If that isn't having an influence on us, I'd like to know what is!

Figure 7: Sumerian Frieze

For example, if we were bred to be slaves of a kind, isn't it interesting that we have the same attitude to our animals? We breed them with little thought to their emotions, feelings, desires or anything else. We impose our desires on them, much as the Annunaki imposed theirs on us.

And what of the strange fixation we have with adornments, precious metals and sex? If the records are exact, then these same traits were those of the aliens. They enjoyed gold jewelry. They altered us to be able to have sex and produce all the time (not the norm!), and they generally showed us the way to behave...belligerently, with little regard to others and to concentrate on outward show rather than inward meaning.

Now, I know these are huge generalizations, but the traits we exhibit as humans must have come from somewhere. I do not subscribe to the theory that these are natural developments of evolution. They are, in many ways, unnatural. Additionally, there is the question of giants, the wee people and the monsters of legend. Could the aliens who created mankind have created the other races of myth and legend? I think it is the case. And we have the Annunaki to thank for them...for us!!

CHAPTER THREE
DIRECT SIGNS OF ALIEN INTERVENTION

For the sake of simplicity in our further discussions, let us call the involvement of unknown person or persons as alien intervention. Certainly in the normal use of the word alien it communicates the idea that they were outsiders.

Once the early civilizations were formed man began to indulge in the second oldest profession, war. These wars were basically for conquest and started the rise of the great empires. As Sitchin asked in his work, "The Wars of Gods and Men[11]" are we merely puppets for the gods or are we cannon fodder? Whichever may be the case there are numerous wars fought by mankind which have been influenced one way or another by "the gods." The empires and religions formed as a result of these contacts might not have formed without them, so it would seem that the Aliens had their own agenda regarding mankind.

While the UFO phenomenon may not have gained popularity until the second half of the 20th Century, there have been many cases documented throughout history that

---

[11] Sitchin, Zacharia, The Wars of Gods and Men: Book III of the Earth Chronicles (The Earth Chronicles), Harper (March 27, 2007)

indicate that the phenomenon occurred often over the centuries.

While one of the more famous ancient UFO sightings could have been the possible sighting in the first chapter of Ezekiel, that was certainly not the only reference to strange flying objects. There have been many references to flying objects or vehicles in the Mahabharata and also various historical paintings over the centuries that clearly indicate that people of that time had either seen or heard of some kind of saucer-shaped craft. In many cases, the depictions in the paintings even suggest some kind of deep-rooted relationship between UFOs and religion.

In the Book of Ezekiel[12], Chapter 1 says "*Behold, a whirlwind came out of the north, a great cloud, and a fire infolding itself, and a brightness was about it, and out of the midst thereof as the color of amber, out of the midst of the fire. Also out of the midst thereof came the likeness of four living creatures. And this was their appearance; they had the likeness of a man. And every one had four faces, and every one had four wings.*" It also speaks of how these living creatures had wheels and how when they "were lifted up from Earth, the wheels were lifted up also."

Figure 8: Early painting of UFO during the Biblical era

---

[12] King James Edition of the Holy Bible.

This account was written six hundred years before Christ. The Greeks and Romans have also written about such things like phantom chariots appearing in the night sky. During the reign of Charlemagne, there were many accounts of "tyrants of the air, and their aerial ships." Charlemagne was so concerned that these reports would frighten the people that those reporting these phenomenon were put to death. There is another case reported in the year 1270 from Bristol, England. A spaceship was seen, which landed and an occupant came down from a ladder and was suffocated in the Earth's atmosphere.

Early Egypt is another civilization which is often belied to have had contact with UFOs. The so-called Tulli Papyrus is oft cited as evidence of visitations to Egypt by "ancient astronauts;" unfortunately, any mention of Alberto Tulli and his alleged papyrus appears to be restricted to popular UFO-related literature.

For example, in "UFOs in History[13]," Samuel Rosenberg describes a number of supposed ancient UFO sightings including one "from a papyrus manuscript found among the papers of the late Professor Alberto Tulli, former director of the Vatican Egyptian Museum." It involves a "UFO sighting sometime during the reign" of Thutmosis III, cited by Trench[14]

According to the story, the former director of the Egyptian Museum at the Vatican, one Professor Alberto Tulli (now deceased) had among his papers "the earliest known record of a fleet of flying saucers written on papyrus

---

[13] Rosenberg, Samuel, UFOs in History,
[14] (Trench, Brinsley Le Poer, The Flying Saucer Story, London: Spearman, 1966).

long, long, ago in ancient Egypt." Though the papyrus was damaged and contained several gaps, a certain Prince Boris de Rachewiltz managed to translate it and declared that the papyrus "was part of the Annals of Thutmose III." Following is a translation of the papyrus:

In the year 22, in the third month of winter, in the sixth hour of the day, the scribes of the House of Life noticed a circle of fire that was coming from the sky [...] From the mouth it emitted a foul breath. It had no head. Its body was one rod long and one rod wide.[1] It had no voice. And from that the hearts of the scribes became confused and they threw themselves down on their bellies [...] then they reported the thing to the Pharaoh [...] His Majesty ordered [...] has been examined [...] and he was meditating on what had happened, that it was recorded in the scrolls of the House of the Life. Now after some days had passed, these things became more and more numerous in the skies. Their splendor exceeded that of the sun and extended to the limits of the four angles of the sky [...] High and wide in the sky was the position from which these fire circles came and went. The army of the Pharaoh looked on with him in their midst. It was after supper. Then these fire circles ascended higher into the sky and they headed toward the south. Fish and birds then fell from the sky. A marvel never before known since the foundation of their land [...] And Pharaoh caused incense to be brought to make peace with Earth[2] [...] and what happened was ordered to be written in the Annals of the House of Life so that it be remembered for all time forward[15].

Early writings also make it clear that these "gods" indulged themselves in the wars of man. The earliest conflict of which a record can be found was in the year 1460 BC.

THUTMOSIS III

Figure 9: Thutmosis III

In this auspicious year Pharaoh Thutmosis III was [16]involved in a conflict with the Nubians. For those not up on their Egyptian history, Thutmose III (sometimes read as Thutmosis or Thutmosis III, or Thothmes in older history works, and meaning Thoth is born) was the sixth Pharaoh of the Eighteenth Dynasty. During the first twenty-two years of Thutmose's reign he was co-regent with his stepmother, Hatshepsut, who was named the pharaoh. While he was shown first on surviving monuments, both were assigned the usual royal names and insignia and neither is given any obvious seniority over the other. He served as the head of her armies.

---

[15] Notes:
1. One rod, or "rod of cord," equals 100 cubits.
2. I.e., the altar sacred to Amon-Ra.

Widely considered a military genius by historians, Thutmose III made 16 raids in 20 years. He was an active expansionist ruler, sometimes called Egypt's greatest conqueror or "the Napoleon of Egypt." He is recorded to have captured 350 cities during his rule and conquered much of the Near East from the Euphrates to Nubia during seventeen known military campaigns. He was the first Pharaoh after Thutmose I to cross the Euphrates, doing so during his campaign against Mitanni. His campaign records were transcribed onto the walls of the temple of Amun at Karnak, and are now transcribed into Urkunden IV. He is consistently regarded as one of the greatest of Egypt's warrior pharaohs, who transformed Egypt into an international superpower by creating an empire that stretched from southern Syria through to Canaan and Nubia. In most of his campaigns his enemies were defeated town by town, until being beaten into submission. The preferred tactic was to subdue a much weaker city or state one at a time resulting in surrender of each fraction until complete domination was achieved.

Much is known about Thutmosis "the warrior", not only because of his military achievements, but also because of his royal scribe and army commander, Thanuny, who wrote about his conquests and reign. The prime reason why Thutmosis was able to conquer such a large number of lands is because of the revolution and improvement in army weapons. When the Hyksos invaded and took over Egypt with more advanced weapons such as horse-drawn chariots, the people of Egypt learned to use these weapons. He encountered only little resistance from neighboring kingdoms, allowing him to expand his realm of influence easily. His army also had carried boats on dry land. These campaigns (17 in 20 years), are inscribed on the inner wall of the great chamber housing the "holy of holies" at the Karnak Temple of Amun. These inscriptions give the most detailed and accurate account of any Egyptian king.

After her death and his later rise to pharaoh of the kingdom, he created the largest empire Egypt had ever seen; no fewer than seventeen campaigns were conducted, and he conquered from Niya in North Syria to the Fourth Cataract of the Nile in Nubia.

Officially, Thutmose III ruled Egypt for almost

Figure 10: Ruins of the Temple of Amun at Jebel Barkal

fifty-four years, and his reign is usually dated from April 24, 1479 BCE to March 11, 1425 BCE; however, this includes the twenty-two years he was co-regent to Hatshepsut—his stepmother and aunt. During the final two years of his reign, he appointed his son and successor, Amenhotep II, as his junior co-regent. When Thutmose III died, he was buried in the Valley of the Kings as were the rest of the kings from this period in Egypt.

Thutmose took one last campaign in his fiftieth regnal year, very late in his life. In 1460 B C, he attacked Nubia, but only went so far as the fourth cataract of the Nile. Although no king of Egypt had ever penetrated so far as he did with an army, previous kings' campaigns had spread Egyptian culture that far already, and the earliest Egyptian document found at Gebel Barkal[17], in fact, comes from three years before Thutmose's campaign.

There is a stela[18] located at Gebel (Jebel) Barkal erected in honor of Thutmosis III[19] which describes what was called a celestial event during his war with the Nubians. According to the stela:

> "A star fell to their South position. It struck those[20] opposed to him. None could stand . . .

---

[17] Also spelled Jebel Barkal it is located in Northern State, Sudan, about 400 kilometers (250 mi) north of Khartoum near Karima. The temple of Amun stands near a large bend of the Nile River, in the region that was called Nubia in ancient times. The Temple of Amun, one of the larger temples at Jebel Barkal, is considered sacred to the local population. Not only was the Amun temple a main center of what at one time was considered to be an almost universal religion, but, along with the other archaeological sites at Jebel Barkal, it was representative of the revival of Egyptian religious values. Up to the middle of the 19th century, the temple was subjected to vandalism, destruction, and indiscriminate plundering, before it came under state protection.

[18] This stela was erected in 1457 in honor of Thutmosis III's victories in Asia.

[19] Translation published in the German Egyptological Journal, *Zeitschrift fur Agyptischen Sprache under Altertumskunde* 69; 24-39 (1933).

[20] Referring to the Nubians.

The star positioned itself above them as if they didn't exist and then they fell upon their own blood. Now the star was behind them (illuminating their faces with fire; no man amongst them could defend themselves, none of them looking back. They had not their horses as (these) had fled into the mountain, frightened. . . Such is the miracle that Amon did for me, his beloved son in order to make the inhabitants of the foreign lands see the power of my majesty."

It would seem that the sky "gods" had a desire that Thutmosis III be victorious over the Nubians. The Egyptians were a progressive society while the Nubians were less so. Did the plans of the sky "gods" call for Egypt to be a might empire at this time in history?

PHAROAH AMENOPHIS IV (A.K.A. AKHENATON)

Akhenaten, meaning "Effective for Aten", known before the fifth year of his reign as Amenhotep IV (sometimes given its Greek form, Amenophis IV, and meaning Amun is Satisfied), was a pharaoh of the Eighteenth dynasty of Egypt who ruled for 17 years and died perhaps in 1336 BC or 1334 BC.

He is especially noted for abandoning traditional Egyptian polytheism and introducing worship centered on the Aten, which is sometimes described as monotheistic or henotheistic. An early inscription likens the Aten to the sun as compared to stars, and later official language avoids calling the Aten a god, giving the solar deity a status above mere gods.

There is a story that Pharaoh Akhenaton had a very unique experience that resulted in his conversion to the worship of Aten and as a result had a tremendous influence on Egyptian history. As found in the inscriptions on the 'Frontier Stela' found at El-Amarna, Amenophis IV was walking along the river bank admiring the splendors of nature one summer morning when he looked up into the sky and saw a *shining disc* descend from the heavens.

Figure 11: Pharaoh Akhenaton

According to the inscription, Amenophis IV heard the voice of the Solar Disc itself[21] tell him that he was to build a new capital for Egypt and give it the name Akhetaton, which translated as *"The Horizon of the Solar Disc."*

Following the orders he had received from the shining disc, Amenophis IV built a new capital for Egypt which became known as the City of Akhetaton. At the same time as the new capital was occupied Akhenaton also introduced a new religion based on the worship of the Solar Disc. Akhenaton became known as the most powerful heretic in ancient history. Could the Solar Disc of

---

[21] Somewhat before the voice from the burning bush that spoke to Moses.

Akhenaton be the UFO of today? Did an Alien race shape the society of ancient Egypt?

ALEXANDER THE GREAT

Alexander III of Macedon (20/21 July 356 – 10/11 June 323 BC), commonly known as Alexander the Great was a king of the Greek kingdom of Macedonia. Born in Pella in 356 BC, Alexander succeeded his father, Philip II to the throne at the age of twenty[22]. He spent most of his ruling years on an unprecedented military campaign through Asia and northeast Africa, until by the age of thirty he had created one of the largest empires of the ancient world, stretching from Greece to Egypt and into present-day Pakistan. He was undefeated in battle and is considered one of history's most successful commanders.

Figure 12: Bust of Alexander the Great

During his youth, Alexander was tutored by the philosopher Aristotle until the age of 16. When he succeeded his father to the throne in 336 BC, after Philip was assassinated, Alexander inherited a strong kingdom and an experienced army. He had been awarded the generalship of Greece and used this authority to launch his

---

[22] There were rumors that he assassinated his father to gain the throne.

father's military expansion plans. In 334 BC, he invaded the Achaemenid Empire, ruled Asia Minor, and began a series of campaigns that lasted ten years. Alexander broke the power of Persia in a series of decisive battles, most notably the battles of Issus and Gaugamela. He subsequently overthrew the Persian King Darius III and conquered the entirety of the Persian Empire. At that point, his empire stretched from the Adriatic Sea to the Indus River.

Figure 13: Philip of Macedonia

Seeking to reach the "ends of the world and the Great Outer Sea", he invaded India in 326 BC, but was eventually forced to turn back at the demand of his troops. Alexander died in Babylon in 323 BC, the city he planned to establish as his capital, without executing a series of planned campaigns that would have begun with an invasion of Arabia. In the years following his death, a series of civil wars tore his empire apart, resulting in several states ruled by the Diadochi, (Alexander's surviving generals and heirs).

While it was not well known there are several instances when UFOs seemed to favor Alexander's efforts in battle. The first recorded incident regarding Alexander the Great and UFO's was recorded in 329 BC[23].

---

[23] Drake, W. Raymond, 'Gods and Spacemen in Greece and Rome',

Alexander decided to invade India and was attempting to cross the river Indus to engage the Indian army when "gleaming silver shields" swooped down and made several passes over the battle. These "gleaming silver shields" had the effect of startling his cavalry horses, causing them to stampede. They also had a similar effect on the enemies' horses and elephants so it was difficult to ascertain whose side these "gleaming silver shields" were on. Nevertheless, after exiting the battle victoriously Alexander decided to not proceed any further into India.

Seven years later, in 332 B C, Alexander was confronted with the greatest challenge of his military career. In his attempt to conquer the Persian Empire he realized that the city of Tyre needed to be captured in order to prevent the Persians from using that port to land an army behind him. The original coastal city of Tyre had been destroyed before and had been rebuilt some distance offshore from its original site[24].

Having no navy, Alexander decided to use the remains of the old city to build a causeway to the new one. It took Alexander six full months to do this and when the task was completed and his troops staged their assault they were easily rebuffed because the walls were too high to quickly scale and too thick to batter down. Not only was the wall too high and too thick, but the causeway was too narrow to allow sufficient troops to launch a massive enough attack to overwhelm the enemy in order to scale the walls.

Sphere, London 1976, pp. 115-116:
[24] Alberto Fenoglio, "Cronistoria su oggetti volanti del passato, - Appunti per una clipeostoria", 'Clypeus' #9, 1st Semester 1966, p. 7

Not only was this a problem for Alexander but apparently a problem for God as well. Both the prophets Ezekiel and Isaiah had spoken of Gods' curse and eventual destruction of Tyre[25]. How was Alexander going to achieve his goal? How was God going to ensure that His prophecy would be fulfilled?

The historical account, recorded by Alexander's chief historian, states that, during an attack of the island city, one of two 'gleaming silver shields' attacked a section of the wall with a 'beam of light' which subsequently caused that section of the wall to fall! Alexander's' men poured through the opening and captured the city[26].

Once again it would seem that mysterious forces took a direct hand in a war between different groups of humans.

A GLOWING PILLAR OF FIRE

Everyone who ever attended Sunday school is familiar with the fact that during the Exodus of the Hebrews from Egypt that God led them through the wilderness with a pillar of fire. It is interesting to note that this was not the only time that God apparently took a direct hand in the affairs of man.

---

[25] Ezekiel Chapters 27 & 28 and Isaiah Chapter 23
[26] Quoting Giovanni Gustavo Droysens Storia di Alessandro il Grande, Alberto Fenoglio, writes in CLYPEUS Anno 111, No 2

In 404 BC in Attica, Greece, Clement of Alexander[27] wrote about a group of refugees being guided by a pillar of fire in the sky. According to Clement of Alexandria, *"When Trasybulus was bringing back the exiles from Phyla, and wished to elude observation, a pillar became his guide as he marched over a trackless region . . . The sky being moonless and stormy, a fire appeared leading the way which have conducted them to safety, left them near Munychia, where is now the altar of the light bringer . . .."*

Figure 14: Pillar of Fire

Once again this event was looked at as the hand of God and an altar was erected in honor of the event when in fact this could have easily been an earthy act by a sky "god." We also see from this event that many of the miracles in the Bible reported by the Hebrews were not unique by any means.

---

[27] Clement of Alexander, Stromata, Book 1, Chapter 24. Cited in The ante-Nicene Fathers, translation of the writing of the Fathers down to AD 325 by Reverend Alexander Roberts and James Donaldson and arranged by A. Cleveland Coxe, Vol. II: Fathers of the Second Century (Edinburgh reprint, 2001)

ANOTHER NEW RELIGION

It is also interesting to note that these sky "gods" were very interested in the religious beliefs of early humans. We saw in ancient Egypt that a Solar Disc caused Akhenaton to create a new religion worshipping the Solar Disc, or what it represented. It is not well known that much the same thing occurred in China.

Figure 15: Buddha

In 44 A D in China, Han Emperor Mingti, who had heard of Buddhism had a vision of a golden figure floating in a halo of light which was interpreted as a flying Apsara (Buddhist angel). Some writers interpreted this event as a dream others as an apparition. Author Arthur Lillie[28] stated that this was a golden man, a spirit named Foe. John Gray calls it a foreign god entering his palace[29].

Whatever the figure may have been, the event was interpreted by the Emperor's wide men, to include Minister Fu Yi, as an appearance by Buddha himself. Consequently an envoy was sent to India to learn about this new religion. He returned with sacred Buddhist texts and paintings as well as Indian priests to explain the teaching of the Buddha to the Emperor. As a result of the interference from an unknown quarter, Buddhism was spread to one of the most populous countries in the world.

---

[28] Lillie, Arthur, Buddhism in Christendom or Jesus the Essene (London: K. Paul, Trench, 1887)
[29] Gray, John Henry, China, a History of the Laws, Manners and Customs of the People (Courier Dover: 2003

So once again, a so called miracle led to the creation of a new religion in the country of China. This once again brings up Clark's third law which states that any science sufficient advanced is indistinguishable from magic. To early man, the powers of the sky "gods" would seem to be magic.

THE CONVERSION OF CONSTANTINE

When Roman Emperor Constantine the Great (reigned 306–337) ruled Rome, Christianity became the dominant religion of the Roman Empire. Historians remain uncertain about Constantine's reasons for favoring Christianity, and theologians and historians have argued about which form of Early Christianity he subscribed to. Although Constantine had been exposed to Christianity by his mother Helena, there is no consensus among scholars as to whether he adopted his mother's Christianity in his youth, or gradually over the course of his life, and he did not receive baptism until shortly before his death.

Figure 16: Constantine's conversion by Reubens

Constantine's conversion was a turning point for Early Christianity, sometimes referred to as the Triumph of the Church, the Peace of the Church or the Constantinian shift. In 313, Constantine and Licinius issued the Edict of

Milan legalizing Christian worship. The emperor became a great patron of the Church and set a precedent for the position of the Christian emperor within the Church and the notion of orthodoxy, Christendom, ecumenical councils and the state church of the Roman Empire declared by edict in 380. He is revered as a saint and is apostolos in the Eastern Orthodox Church and Oriental Orthodox Church for his example as a "Christian monarch." What is interesting is how this conversation came about. It happened according to legend just before the Battle of Milvian Bridge.

Eusebius of Caesarea and other Christian sources record that Constantine experienced a dramatic event in 312 at the Battle of Milvian Bridge, after which Constantine claimed the emperorship in the West. According to these sources, Constantine looked up to the sun before the battle and saw a cross of light above it, and with it a large number of what he described as shields upon which were seen the Greek words "Εν Τούτῳ Νίκα" (~in this sign you shall conquer!), often rendered in the Latin "in hoc signo vinces"). Constantine commanded his troops to adorn their shields with a Christian symbol (the Chi-Rho), and thereafter they were victorious.

Following the battle, the new emperor ignored the altars to the gods prepared on the Capitoline and did not carry out the customary sacrifices to celebrate a general's victorious entry into Rome, instead heading directly to the imperial palace. Most influential people in the empire, however, especially high military officials, had not converted to Christianity and still participated in the traditional religions of Rome; Constantine's rule exhibited at least a willingness to appease these factions. The Roman coins minted up to eight years after the battle still bore the images of Roman gods. The monuments he first commissioned, such as the Arch of Constantine, contained no reference to Christianity.

Once again a mysterious object in the sky had a direct influence over the affairs of man. It would seem that these mysterious powers in the sky spend an inordinate amount of time influencing the efforts of man o achieve their desires.

CHAPTER FOUR
UFOS IN RELIGION

While there is no doubt that the sky "gods" went to great lengths to influence early man and his religions, there are a number of other forms of religion that seem to be built almost totally around the idea that UFOs and aliens have visited this planet.

A UFO religion is any religion in which the existence of extraterrestrial (ET) entities operating unidentified flying objects (UFOs) are an element of belief. Typically, adherents of such religions believe the ETs to be interested in the welfare of humanity which either already is, or eventually will become, part of a preexisting ET civilization. Others may incorporate ETs into a more supernatural worldview in which the UFO occupants are more akin to angels than physical aliens; this distinction may be a little blurred within the overall subculture. These religions have their roots in the tropes of early science fiction (especially space opera) and weird fiction writings, in ufology, and in the subculture of UFO sightings and alien abduction stories. Scientology is the largest UFO related religion in the world followed by Raelism.

Some adherents believe that the arrival or rediscovery of alien civilizations, technologies and spirituality will enable humans to overcome their current ecological, spiritual and social problems. Issues such as hatred, war, bigotry, poverty and so on are said to be resolvable through the use of superior alien technology and spiritual abilities. Such belief systems are also described as millenarian in their outlook.

UFO religions naturally have developed first in such countries as the United States, Canada, France, the United Kingdom and Japan as the concept presumes the cultural context of a society technologically advanced enough to conceive of ET as such and one in which religion of any kind is not discouraged or suppressed. The term "flying saucers" and the popular notion of the UFO originated in 1947. The 1950s saw the creation of UFO religions, with the advent of the purported contactees.

In this chapter we will review some of these UFO related religions;

- **Aetherius Society**

The Aetherius Society was founded in the United Kingdom in 1955. Its founder, George King, claimed to have been contacted telepathically by an alien intelligence called Aetherius, who represented an "Interplanetary Parliament." According to Aetherians, their society acts as a vehicle through which "Cosmic Transmissions of advanced metaphysical significance" can be disseminated to the rest of humanity. These "transmissions" were recorded on magnetic reel-to-reel tape by persons present during each "telepathic transmission" as George King sat in a state of "Samadhi" and the "transmission" was "delivered" via his voice box. In 1956 and 1957, and on occasion before a public audience, several of these "transmissions" forecast flying saucer activity in specific parts of the world on certain dates (You Are Responsible! Aetherius Society 1961). Shortly after these dates, newspapers, such as the Sunday Times and The Daily Telegraph, reported sightings which coincided with the dates and locations forecast in these "transmissions".(citation?) As a spiritual teacher, George King taught certain yoga practices, spiritual healing, Eastern mantra and "dynamic prayer"—tools for spiritual self-advancement and service to the world—which the Aetherius Society is principally based upon.

- **Church of the SubGenius**
Founded in 1979 with the publication of SubGenius Pamphlet #1 by Ivan Stang and Philo Drummond, the Church of the SubGenius has been known as a "parody religion" due to its extensive use of comedy and parody. In spite of this, the organization claims over 10,000 followers worldwide who have paid $30 to become "ordained SubGenius ministers", and it has been embraced by many skeptic and atheist groups. With the

Figure 17: Logo for Church of the Subgenius

publication of The Book of the SubGenius in 1983, the Church of the SubGenius prophesied that its founder, J.R. "Bob" Dobbs, was in contact with an extraterrestrial race called the Xists ("X-ists"), and these Xists were scheduled to launch a worldwide invasion of Earth on July 5, 1998. (See also: X-Day (Church of the SubGenius)) The day of the scheduled invasion came and went without an appearance by the Xists, but church members remain unconvinced. The church now holds annual "X-Day" celebrations on July 5 of every year. The church also claims that its members are not entirely human, having descended from the Yeti.

- **Heaven's Gate**

The Heaven's Gate group achieved notoriety in 1997 when one of its founders convinced 38 followers to commit mass suicide. Members reportedly believed themselves to be aliens, awaiting a spaceship that would arrive with Comet Hale-Bopp. The suicide was undertaken in the apparent belief that their souls would be transported onto the spaceship, which they thought was hiding behind the comet. They underwent elaborate preparations for their trip, including purchasing and wearing matching shoes. For a time, group members lived in a darkened house where

Figure 18: Heaven's Gate Logo

they would simulate the experience they expected to have during their long journey in outer space.

- **Universal Industrial Church of the New World Comforter**

The Universal Industrial Church of the New World Comforter is a UFO religion founded in 1973 by Allen Michael.

In 1947, Allen Noonan was a pictorial sign painter in Long Beach, California, who that year claimed to have an encounter with Galactic Space Beings. While painting a signboard he said he was beamed up into a Mothership. He then changed his name to Allen Michael.

He claimed to have physically encountered a flying saucer in 1954 at Giant Rock in the Mojave Desert of California. During the Summer of Love, he began the One World Family Commune with a vegan restaurant on the northeast corner of Haight and Scott streets in San Francisco, California, called the Here and Now. Seven similar restaurants followed.

His communal group lived in two large houses during the early 1970s in Berkeley, California. In 1969, the commune established a vegan restaurant in a much larger space on Telegraph Avenue and Haste Street in Berkeley and the name of the restaurant was changed to the One World Family Natural Food Center. They published a vegetarian cookbook called Cosmic Cookery. There was a large mural on the side of the restaurant painted by Allen Michael that had written above it the phrase Farmers, Workers, Soldiers Unite —

The People's Spiritual Reformation 1776 - 1976! The farmer was holding a pitchfork, the worker was holding a hammer, and the soldier was holding a gun, and they had their arms around each other's shoulders. Above the three were three flying saucers coming in for a landing.

In 1973, Allen Michael founded "The Universal Industrial Church of the New World Comforter" and published the first volume of his channeled revelations, The Everlasting Gospel. In 1975, the church headquarters and the vegetarian restaurant relocated to Stockton, California. Allen Noonan ran for president of the United States in the 1980 and 1984 elections on the Utopian Synthesis Party ticket.

- **Nation of Islam**

The Nation of Islam subscribes to the belief that UFOs are man-made machines that are piloted not by extraterrestrial beings, but by humans. It is believed that these machines will have a hand in the Day of Judgment. Its late leader Elijah Muhammad claimed that the Biblical Book of Ezekiel

Figure 19: Nation of Islam

describes a "Mother Plane" or great "Wheel". Elijah reported in his books that his mentor, Wallace Fard Muhammad, claimed that there was hidden technology on the Earth which selected scientists all around the world are secretly aware of. Fard explained that he had had a huge "Mother Plane" or "Wheel" constructed on the island of Nippon (Japan) in 1929. The movement's current leader, Louis Farrakhan, describes the "Mother Plane" thus:

The Honorable Elijah Muhammad told us of a giant Motherplane that is made like the universe, spheres within spheres. White people call them unidentified flying objects (UFOs). Ezekiel, in the Old Testament, saw a wheel that looked like a cloud by day but a pillar of fire by night. The Hon. Elijah Muhammad said that that wheel was built on the island of Nippon, which is now called Japan, by some of the original scientists. It took 15 billion dollars in gold at that time to build it. It is made of the toughest steel. America does not yet know the composition of the steel used to make an instrument like it. It is a circular plane, and the Bible says that it never makes turns. Because of its circular nature it can stop and travel in all directions at speeds of thousands of miles per hour. He said there are 1,500 small wheels in this mother wheel which is a half mile by a half mile (800 by 800 m). This Mother Wheel is like a small human built planet. Each one of these small planes carries three bombs.

- **Raëlism**

The International Raëlian Movement has been described as "the largest UFO religion in the world." Raëlians believe that scientifically advanced extraterrestrials, known as the Elohim, created life on Earth through genetic engineering, and that a combination of human cloning and "mind transfer" can ultimately provide eternal life. Past religious teachers, like Jesus, Buddha and Muhammad are said to have been sent by these scientifically advanced extraterrestrials to teach humanity. The Elohim are said to be planning a future visit to complete their revelation and education of humanity.

Figure 20: Raeliam

Raëlian Priest Thomas said on this topic, *"The difference between Raëlians and Heaven's Gate and Jim Jones etc., is that the others destructively believed in a God who would give them a better life after death, just like most believers in a monotheistic religion do today, and hence the risk for suicide chasing afterlife rewards ... as Raëlians we want the best right now in our life, who would want to die now in that scenario with all those pleasures to enjoy? Raëlians believe in enjoying life now, with happiness and laughter."*

- **Scientology**

Scientology has been discussed in the context of UFO religions in UFO Religions by Christopher Partridge, The Encyclopedic Sourcebook of UFO Religions by James R. Lewis, and UFO Religion: Inside Flying Saucer Cults and Culture by Gregory Reece. Stories of extraterrestrial civilizations and interventions in past lives form a part of the belief system of Scientology. The most well-known story publicized and held up to ridicule by critics is that of Xenu, the ruler of the Galactic Confederacy who is said to have brought billions of frozen people to Earth 75 million years ago and placed them near a number of volcanoes, and dropped hydrogen bombs into them, thus killing the entire population in an effort to solve overpopulation. The spirits of these people were then captured by Xenu and mass implanted with numerous suggestions and then "packaged" into clusters of spirits.

Figure 21: Scientology

From the early 1950s onwards, Scientology's founder, L. Ron Hubbard, published a number of books, lectures and other works describing what he termed "space opera".

Scientology teaches that all humans have experienced innumerable past lives, including lives in ancient advanced extraterrestrial societies, such as Helatrobus and the Marcabians. Traumatic memories from these past lives are said to be the cause of many present-day physical and mental ailments. Scientologists also believe that human beings possess superhuman powers which cannot be restored until they have been fully rehabilitated as spiritual beings through the practice of "auditing", using methods set out by Hubbard in his various works.

According to Hubbard, when thetans (the Scientology term for a human being) die they go to a "landing station" on the planet Venus, where they are re-implanted and are programmed to "forget" their previous lifetimes, thus causing amnesia. The Venusians then "capsule" each thetan and send them back to Earth to be dumped into the ocean off the coast of California; whereupon, each thetan searches for a new body to inhabit. To avoid these inconveniences, Hubbard advised Scientologists to simply refuse to go to Venus after their death.

- **Unarius Academy of Science**

Figure 22: Unarius Academy of Science

Founded by Ernest L. Norman and his wife, Ruth, in 1954, the Unarians are a group headquartered in El Cajon, California, who believe that, through the use of fourth dimensional physics, they are able to communicate with supposed advanced intelligent beings that allegedly exist on higher frequency planes. Unarians believe in past lives and hold that the Solar System was once inhabited by ancient interplanetary civilizations.

- **Universe people**

The Universe people or Cosmic people of light powers (Czech: Vesmírní lidé sil světla) is a Czech movement centered around Ivo A. Benda. Its belief system is based upon the existence of extraterrestrial civilizations communicating with Benda and other "contacters" since October 1997 telepathically and later by direct personal contact. According to Benda, those civilizations operate a fleet of spaceships led by Ashtar (sometimes written Ashtar Sheran) orbiting and closely watching the Earth, helping the good and waiting to transport the followers into another dimension. The Universe People teaching incorporates various elements from ufology (some foreign "contacters" are credited, though often also renounced after a time as misguided or deceptive), Christianity (Jesus was a "fine-vibrations" being) and conspiracy theories (forces of evil are supposed to plan compulsory chipping of the populace).

Figure 23: Universe People

- **UFOs in other religions**

The Theosophical guru Benjamin Creme claims that the Messiah figure he refers to as Maitreya, who, he teaches, will soon declare himself publicly, is in telepathic contact with the space brothers in their flying saucers. Creme subscribes to the view that Nordic aliens from Venus pilot flying saucers from a civilization on Venus hundreds of millions of years in advance of ours that exists on the etheric plane of Venus. These flying saucers are capable of stepping down the level of vibration of themselves and their craft to the slower level of vibration of the atoms of the physical plane (Creme accepts George Adamski's UFO sightings as valid). According to Creme, the Venusians have mother ships up to four miles long. It is also believed by the Theosophists in general as well as Creme in particular that the governing deity of Earth, Sanat Kumara (who is believed to live in a city called Shamballa located above the Gobi desert on the etheric plane of Earth), is a Nordic alien who originally came from Venus 18,500,000 years ago. The followers of Benjamin Creme believe there is regular flying saucer traffic between Venus and Shamballah and that crop circles are mostly caused by flying saucers.

Figure 24: Benjamin Creme

The Ascended Master Teachings are a group of religions based on Theosophy. In the traditional Ascended Master Teachings of Guy Ballard and Elizabeth Clare Prophet, no mention is made of UFOs or flying saucers. However, the Ascended Master Teachings teacher Joshua David Stone in his teachings began, beginning in 1993, to refer to Ashtar, believed by some UFO enthusiasts to be the commander of a flying saucer fleet called the "Ashtar Galactic Command" that operates near Earth (manned mostly by Venusians), as a Master along with the more traditional ascended masters. He continued to include "Ashtar" on his list of ascended masters that he mentioned he received dictations from when speaking at his yearly Wesak Festival Mount Shasta gatherings that began to be held in 1996. Stone also taught that the Master Jesus, under his "galactic" name Sananda, sometimes rides with "Commander Ashtar" in his flying saucer fleet.

A neo-Nazi esoteric Nazi Gnostic sect headquartered in Vienna, Austria, called the Tempelhofgesellschaft, founded in the early 1990s, teaches what it calls a form of Marcionism. They distribute pamphlets claiming that the Aryan race originally came to Atlantis from the star Aldebaran (this

Figure 25: Templehofgesellschaft

information is supposedly based on "ancient Sumerian manuscripts"). They maintain that the Aryans from Aldebaran derive their power from the Vril energy of the Black Sun. They teach that since the Aryan race is of extraterrestrial origin it has a divine mission to dominate all the other races. It is believed by adherents of this religion that an enormous space fleet is on its way to Earth from Aldebaran which, when it arrives, will join forces with the "Nazi Flying Saucers from Antarctica" to establish the Western Imperium.

The New Message from God claims that aliens are on Earth to take advantage of imminent, global environmental collapse, stating that, "humanity is now facing competition from beyond the world, intervention from races beyond the world who seek to take advantage of a weak and divided humanity, who seek to benefit from the decline of human civilization."

There is no doubt that UFOs have had a tremendous impact on the religious beliefs of a large portion of the earth's population. Their influence can be seen in every religious text on the planet as well as the formations of these cultish religions in this chapter.

CHAPTER FIVE
EVIDENCE OF EARLY ADVANCED CIVILIZATIONS

There are quite a number of lost cities to be found in South America that long pre-date even the natives of South America. Many of these cities are so old that there are not even legends among the natives as to who may have built the cities or what happened to those that lived in the cities. It is also interesting to note that many of these cities are designed in ways totally foreign to the building practices of the known early peoples of the region.

The ancient Mayans had contact with alien visitors

Figure 26: Astronomical frieze

who left behind evidence of their existence and supposedly some lost cities according many legends from pre-history.

WHAT IS A LOST CITY?

Lost city is a term that can be used to a human settlement that which fell into terminal decline and became extensively or completely uninhabited. The location of many of these cities had been forgotten, but some have been rediscovered and studied extensively by scientists. Recently abandoned cities or cities whose location was never in question might be referred to as ruins or ghost towns. The search for such lost cities by European explorers and adventurers in the Americas, Africa and in Southeast Asia from the 15th century onwards eventually led to the development of archaeology.

Figure 27: Typical mythical lost city

It is also interesting to note that some of these cities are reportedly the repositories of advanced technology or show signs of having been very advanced prior to being lost to history. This could account for any stories of alien contact; the aliens were actually survivors of a lost, advanced civilization.

Lost cities generally fall into two broad categories: those where no knowledge of the city existed until the time of its rediscovery, and those where location has been lost but knowledge of its existence has been retained in myths, legends, or historical records[30].

Cities may become lost for a variety of reasons including natural disasters, economic or social upheaval, or war.

The Incan capital city of Vilcabamba was destroyed and depopulated during the Spanish conquest of Peru in 1572. The Spanish did not rebuild the city and the location went unrecorded and was forgotten until it was rediscovered through a detailed examination of period letters and documents.

Troy was a city located in northwest Anatolia in what is now Turkey. It is best known for being the focus of the Trojan War described in the Greek Epic Cycle and especially in the Iliad, one of the two epic poems attributed to Homer. Repeatedly destroyed and rebuilt, the city slowly declined and was abandoned in the Byzantine era. Buried by time, the city was consigned to the realm of legend until the location was first excavated in the 1860s.

Other settlements are lost with few or no clues to their decline. Malden Island located in the central Pacific, was deserted when first visited by Europeans in 1825, but the unsuspected presence of ruined temples and the remains of other structures found on the island indicate that a population of Polynesians had lived there for perhaps several generations some centuries earlier. Prolonged

---

[30] http://en.wikipedia.org/wiki/Lost_city

drought seems the most likely explanation for their demise and the remote nature of the island meant few visitors.

CITIES OF LEGEND
Some cities which are considered lost are (or may be) places of legend.
- Arthurian Camelot
- Kitezh, Russia - Legendary underwater city which supposedly may be seen in good weather.
- Lyonesse
- Ys - Legendary city on the western coast of France.
- The Seven Cities of Gold
- Shambhala
- El Dorado
- Atlantis
- Vineta – Legendary city somewhere at the Baltic coast of Germany or Poland.
- Ciudad de los Cesares - City of the Caesars, A legendary city in Patagonia, never found. Also variously known as City of the Patagonia, Wandering City, Trapalanda or Trapananda, Lin Lin or Elelín.
- Paititi – A legendary city and refuge in the rainforests where Peru, Bolivia and Brazil meet.
- Otuken - legendary capital city of Gokturks in Turkic mythology.
- Ai - important city in the Hebrew Bible.
- Sodom and Gomorrah
- Iram of the Pillars – Lost Arabian city in the Empty Quarter.

- Lost City of Z - A city allegedly located in the jungles of the Matto Grosso region of Brazil, was said to have been seen by the British explorer Col. Percy Harrison Fawcett sometime prior to World War I.

Others, such as Troy and Bjarmaland, having once been considered legendary, are now known to have existed.

LOST CITY OF Z

However, not every legendary lost city is a fantasy. There is every sign that what has been called the Lost City of Z may well be a reality. First discovered by a Portuguese Expedition in the 1700s this lost city seems to be from a civilization of which no one has ever heard. The leader of the survivors of that expedition wrote a report for the Viceroy of Brazil and it is referred to as Manuscript 512. What follows is an English translation of that manuscript. English Translation of Manuscript 512

Figure 28; Colonel Percy Fawcett who disappeared in 1925 looking for the Lost City of Z

Background info: In 1925 Colonel Percy Harrison Fawcett, his son Jack Fawcett and Raleigh Rimmell entered the Amazon jungle to search for a Lost City that for some reason he strangely named Z. It was to be his ninth and final expedition as they were never seen or heard of again.

Figure 29: Photo at Dead Horse Camp

It seems Fawcett based much of his belief of a Lost City on an old document he found in the library archives at Rio de Janeiro in 1920. Labelled Manuscript 512, it arrived in Rio de Janeiro in 1754 and is about a Portuguese expedition into the Amazon interior in 1743.

Having already become intrigued with the rumors local Indians had told him about a lost city in the uncharted areas of the jungle, the information he read in the old document no doubt convinced him they were true.

Although Fawcett had great admiration for the Amazonian Indians and repeatedly refused to use force against them, even when attacked himself, he was not immune to the endemic racism of his time. He did not believe that the native Indians themselves had created this great city, but no doubt some lost European tribe, the Phoenicians or the Lost Tribes of Israel, had built the city before intermarrying with the Indians. He said he had seen white or fair skinned Indians on his travels through the jungle.

Evidence of Alien Contact

Presumably worried that someone would steal his chance of a great discovery, Fawcett was given to secrecy and cryptic notes where the Lost City was concerned. Probably the reason he named in the nondescript 'Z'. He theorized this Lost City was located in the Matto Grosso region of the Brazilian Amazon Jungle, between the Upper Xingu and Tapajos rivers. This in part seems to be true as he was last seen alive in this area at a place he named Dead Horse Camp. He shot a lame horse here on a previous expedition. When he entered the jungle in May 1925, never to be seen or heard of again, no one knows his exact heading or ultimate destination, or even if he ever discovered his lost City of Z.

After reading Manuscript 512, it is plain to see why it convinced Colonel Fawcett that a Lost City did indeed exist somewhere in the Amazon jungle. Put yourself in Fawcett's frame of mind at the time, after hearing stories from some of the indigenous tribes about a Lost City in the jungle, and then reading the manuscript. Would you think the same as him?

Although the Manuscript describes the 'city' in great detail, frustratingly it doesn't include a specific location

Please note: Due to parts of the manuscript being eaten by the Copied worm, parts of the text has been lost. This is indicated by ....

Historical Relation of a hidden and great city of ancient date, without inhabitants, that was discovered in the year 1753.

In America............nos interiores (we inland).......contiguous aos (next to the)....Mestre de Can (Master of Can)............................and his band

Figure 30: Matto Grasso, Brazil

(commitiva), having for ten years journeyed in the wilds (sertoes) to see if we could locate the famous silver mines of the Great Moribecca (who, by the wickedness (culpa) of a Governor, was not granted letters patent, because the Governor wanted to take the silver mines for himself and the glory thereof, and he, the Moribecca, was kept prisoner in Bahia, till he died, which was done to worm out of him the location of the silver mines. This account came to Rio de Janeiro, in the beginning of the year 1754..."

"After long and wearisome wanderings, incited by the insatiable lust for gold, and almost lost cordillera of mountains, so high that they drew near the ethereal region (chegavdo a regido etherea), and served as a throne of the winds, under the stars; their lustre, from afar, excited our wonder and admiration, principally when the sun shining on them turned to fires the crystals of which the rocks were composed. The view was so beautiful that none could take their eyes from the reflections. It began to rain before we came near enough to take note of these crystalline marvels, and we saw above...The spectacle was bare and sterile rocks,

the waters precipitated themselves from the heights, foaming white, like snow, struck and turned to fire by the rays of the sun, like thunder-bolts. Delighted by the pleasing vistas of that....blended....shone and glistered....of the waters and the tranquility....of the day or weather (do tempo), we determined to investigate these prodigious marvels of nature, spread out before us, at the foot of the mountains, without hindrance of forests or rivers that would make it difficult for us to cross them. But when we walked round the foot of the cordillera we found no open way or pass into the recesses of these Alps and Pyrenees of Brazil. So there resulted for us, from this disappointment, an inexplicable sadness.

"*We grew weary and intended to retrace our steps, the next day, when it came to pass that one of our negroes, gathering dried sticks, saw a white deer (hum veado branco), and, by that accident, as it fled away, he discovered a road between two sierras, that appeared to have been made by man and not the work of Nature. We were made joyful by this discovery and we started to ascend the road, but found a great boulder that had fallen and broken all to pieces at a spot where, we judged, a paved way (calcada) had been violently upheaved in some far-off day. We spent a good three hours in the ascent of that ancient road, being fascinated by the crystals, at which we marvelled, as they blazed and scintillated in many flashing colours from the rocks. On the summit of the pass through the mountain, we came to a halt.*

"Thence, spread out before our eyes, we saw in the open plain (campo raso) greater spectacles (demonstracoes) for our vision of admiration and wonder. At the distance of about a league, as we judged, we saw a great city (povoacao grande), and we estimated, by the extent and sight of it, that it must be some city of the court of Brazil; we at once descended the road towards the valley, but with great caution.....would be, in like case, ordered to explore......by quality and...............if so well as they had noticed........smokes (fumines (?)), that being one of the evident signs or vestiges of the place (povoacao).

"Two days we waited, wondering whether to send out scouts, for the end we longed for, and all alone, we waited till daybreak, in great doubt and confused perplexity of mind, trying to guess if the city had any people in it. But it became clear to us there were no inhabitants. An Indian of our bandeirantes determined, after two days of hesitation, to risk his life in scouting by way of precaution; but he returned, amazing us by affirming he had met no one; nor could discover foot-steps or traces of any person whatever. This so confounded us that we could not believe we saw dwellings or buildings, and so, all the scouts (os exploradores) in a body, followed in the steps of the Indian......."

"They now saw for themselves that it was true the great city was uninhabited. We, all, therefore, now decided to enter the place, our arms *ready for instant use, at daybreak. At our entry we met none to bar our way, and we encountered no other road except the one which led to the dead city. This, we entered under three arches (arcos) of great height, the middle arch being the greatest, and the two of the sides being but small; under the great and principal arch we made out letters, which we could not copy, owing to their great height above the ground.*

"Behind, was a street as wide as the three arches, with, here and there, houses of very large size, whose facades of sculptured stone, already blackened with age; alone........inscriptions, all open to the day (todos aberias).....decreases of.......observing, by the regularity and symmetry with their terraces open to the day, without one tile; for the houses had, some of them, burnt floors; others large flagstones.

"We went, with fear and trembling, into some of the houses, and in none did we find vestiges of furniture, or moveable objects by which, or whose use, we might guess at the sort of people who had dwelt therein. The houses were all dark, in the interior, and hardly could the light of day penetrate, even at its dimmest, and, as the vaults gave back the echoes of our speech, the sound of our voices terrified us. We went on into the strange city and we came on a road (street: rua) of great length, and a well set-out plaza (uma praca regular), besides, in it, and in the middle of the plaza a column of black stone of extraordinary grandeur, on whose summit

was a statue of a man (homen ordinario: not a god, or demi-god) with a hand on the left hip and right arm out-stretched, pointing with the index finger to the north pole; and each corner of the said plaza is an obelisk like those among the Romans, but now badly damaged, and cleft as by thunderbolts.

"On the right side of the plaza is a superb building, as it were the principal town-house of some great lord of the land; there is a great hall (saldo) at the entrance, but still being awed and afraid, not all of us entered in the hou.......being so many and the retre......ed to form some.........ed we encounter a.....mass of extraordin........it was difficult for him to lift it................

"The bats were so numerous that they fluttered in swarms round the faces of our people, and made so much noise that it was astonishing. Above the principal portico of the street is a figure in half-relief, cut out of the same stone, and naked from the waist upward, crowned with laurel, representing a person of youthful years, without beard, with a girdle (banda) around him, and an under-garment (um fraldelim) open in front at the waist, underneath the shield (escudo) of this figure are certain characters, now badly defaced by time, but we made out the following:

"On the left side of the plaza is another totally ruined building, and the vestiges remaining well show that it was a temple, because of the still standing side of its magnificent facade, and certain naves of stone, standing entire. It covers much *ground, and in the ruined halls are seen works of beauty, with other statues of portraits inlaid in the stone, with crosses of various shapes, curves (arches (?) corvos) and many other figures that would take too long to describe here.*

"Beyond this building a great part of the city lies completely in ruins, and buried under great masses of earth, and frightful crevasses in the ground, and in all this expanse of utter desolation there is seen no grass, herb, tree, or plant produced by nature, but only mountainous heaps of stone, some raw (that is, unworked), others worked and carved, whereby we understood........ they ...... because again among...... of...... corpses that.......... and part of this unhappy............ and overthrown, perhaps, by some earthquake.

"Opposite this plaza, there runs very swiftly a most deep (caudaloso) and wide river, with spacious banks, that were very pleasing to the eye: it was eleven to twelve fathoms in width, without reckoning the windings, clear and bared at its banks of groves, as of trees and of the trunks that are often brought down in floods. We sounded its depths and found the deepest parts to be fifteen or sixteen fathoms. The country beyond consists wholly of very green and flourishing fields, and so blooming with a variety of flowers that it seemed as if Nature, more attentive to these parts, had laid herself out to create the most beautiful gardens of Flora: we gazed, too, in admiration and astonishment at certain lakes covered with wild

rice plants from which we profited, and also at the innumerable flocks of geese that bred in these fertile plains (campos); but it would have been difficult to sound their depths with the hand, in the absence of a sounding-rod.

"Three days we journeyed down the river, and we stumbled on a cataract (uma catadupa) of such roaring noise and commotion of foaming waters that we supposed the mouths of the much talked of Nile could not have made more trouble or booming, or offered more resistance to our further progress. Afterwards, the river spreads out so much from this cascade that it appears to be a great Ocean (qui parece a grande Oceano). It is all full of peninsulas, covered with green grass, with groves of trees, here and there, that make......... pleas................. Here, we find....................... for want of it, we.............................. the variety of game............... many created beings without hunters to hunt and chase them.

"On the eastern side of this cataract, we found various subterranean hollows (subcavoes) and frightful holes, and made trial of their depths with many ropes; but, after many attempts we were never able to plumb their depths. We found, besides, certain broken stones, and (lying) on the surface of the ground, thrown down, with bars of silver (crevadas de prata) that may have been extracted from the mines, abandoned at the time.

"Among these caverns (furnas) we saw some covered with a great flagstone, with the following

figures cut into it that suggest a great mystery. They are as follows:

"Over the portico of the temple, we saw, besides, the following forms:

"Distant a cannon-shot from the abandoned city is a building like a country house (casa de campo), with a frontage of 250 feet. It is approached by a great portico, from which a stairway built with a door communicating with the said great chamber. Each room has its waterspout (or fountain: bica de agua)...................... the which water meets.................. in the exterior courtyard..............colonnades in the sur............ squared and fashioned by hand, overhung with the characters following:

"Thence, leaving that marvel, we went down to the banks of the river to see whether we could find gold, and without difficulty, we saw, on the surface of the soil, a fine trail promising great riches, as well of gold, as of silver: we marveled that this place had been abandoned by those who had formerly inhabited it; for, with all our careful investigations and great diligence we had met no person, in this wilderness, who might tell us of this deplorable marvel of an abandoned city, whose ruins, statues and grandeur, attested its former populous ness, wealth, and its flourishing in the centuries past; whereas, today, it is inhabited by

> **EXPLORERS LOST IN AMAZON JUNGLE**
>
> **Possible News of Men Not Heard of Since 1925**
>
> It was officially confirmed in London yesterday that the British Consul at Sao Paulo has received a report that Colonel P. H. Fawcett, the British explorer, who disappeared in the Amazon jungle seven years ago, is still alive. A Swiss hunter has told the Consul that he has seen Colonel Fawcett recently, and that the Colonel is held captive by an Amazon tribe. The Consul has been officially requested to telegraph further details to London.
>
> The news from Sao Paulo may throw light on a mystery that several explorers had tried to pierce. Colonel Fawcett, with his son and a companion, disappeared in May, 1925, when exploring the Central Brazil jungle region. In 1927 there was a report that the Fawcetts had been seen alive, but other evidence indicated that they were murdered by jungle-dwellers.

Figure 31: News Article About Fawcett

swallows, bats, rats and foxes, that, fed on the innumerable swarms of hens and geese, have become bigger than a pointer dog. The rats have the tails so short that they leap like fleas and do not run or walk, as they do in other places.

"At this place, the band separated, and one company, joined by others, journeyed forward, and, after nine days long marching, saw, at a distance, on the bank of a great bay (enseada) into which the river spreads, a canoe with some white persons, with long, flowing, black hair, dressed like Europeans................a gunshot fired as a signal to.................... for they had escaped. They had.........................shaggy and wild..................... their hair is plaited and they wear clothes.

"One of our company, named Joao Antonio, found In the ruins of a house a piece of gold money, of spherical shape, greater than our Brazilian coin of 6,400 reis: on one side was an image, or figure of a kneeling youth; on the other, a bow, a crown, and an arrow (setta), of which coins we doubted not to have found many in the abandoned city; since it was *overthrown by an earthquake, which gave no time, so sudden was its onset, to take away precious objects; but it needs a very powerful arm to turn over the rubbish, accumulated in so many long years, as we saw.*

"This news is sent to your Honour from the interior of the province of Bahia and from the rivers Para-oacu and Una, and assuring you that we shall give information to no person, whatsoever; for we judge the villages are empty of people and boat owners. But I have given to your Honour the mine we have discovered, reminded of the great deal that is owed to you.

"Supposing that from our band, one of our company went forth, at this time, with a different pretense.....he may, with great harm to your Honour, abandon his poverty and and come to use these great things for his own benefit, taking great care to bribe that Indian (therefore), so as to spoil his purpose and lead your Honour to these great treasures, etc...............................would find, in the entrances..........flagsones.............."

These strange characters were engraved on the great stones, sealing the vault of treasure that the baneiristas could not open.

This completes the fascinating manuscript by the bandeiristas of Minas Geracs that inspired many explorers to search for the lost city. Colonel P. H. Fawcett found that fourteen out of the twenty-four characters inscribed on the pillars and porticoes recorded in the South American manuscript were identical with those he accidentally discovered in the jungle forest of Ceylon. When he got back to civilization he took a copy of the inscriptions to a learned Sinhalese priest, who told him that the writing was a form of Asoka, of the old Asoka Buddhists, in a cypher which only those ancient priests understood. Experts surmise that the bizarre inscriptions record the caching, in a time of great dearth, or famine, of an immense treasure that would be thousands of years old.

Fawcett was not the only explorer to act on the Information in Manuscript 512, Richard Burton also ventured forth into the Amazon jungle. He wrote a book about his exploration called, Explorations of the Highlands of Brazil: With a Full Account of the Gold & Diamond Mines.

So as you can see there is some fair decent evidence that the Lost City of Z may well exist in the jungles of South America. Having spent several years in those jungles, I can attest to the fact that the jungle quickly covers everything, making it very hard to find anything thing after any appreciable period of time

CHAPTER SIX
ABDUCTIONS AND VISITATIONS BY ALIENS

Over the last forty years or so there has been much discussion about the abduction of humans by aliens. The terms alien abduction or abduction phenomenon describe *"subjectively real memories of being taken secretly against one's will by apparently nonhuman entities and subjected to complex physical and psychological procedures"*. People claiming to have been

Figure 32: The entity described by many abductees

abducted are usually called "abductees" or "experiencers[31]".

Due both the unbelievable nature of the experience as well as the scarcity of objective physical evidence, most scientists and mental health professionals dismiss the phenomenon as "deception, suggestibility (fantasy-proneness, hypnotizability, false memory syndrome), personality, sleep paralysis, psychopathology, psychodynamics [and] environmental factors".

However, the late Prof. John E. Mack[32], a respected Harvard University psychiatrist, devoted a substantial amount of time to investigating such cases and eventually concluded that the only phenomenon in psychiatry that adequately explained the patients' symptoms in several of the most compelling cases was posttraumatic stress disorder. As he noted at the time, this would imply that the patient genuinely believed that the remembered frightening incident had really occurred.

Skeptic Robert Sheaffer sees similarity between the aliens depicted in early science fiction films, in particular, *Invaders From Mars*, and some of those reported to have actually abducted people.

Typical claims involve being subjected to a forced medical examination that emphasizes their reproductive system. Abductees sometimes claim to have been warned against environmental abuse and the dangers of nuclear weapons. While many of these claimed encounters are

---

[31] http://en.wikipedia.org/wiki/Alien_abduction
[32] Mack, J. E. (1994). <u>Abduction: Human Encounters with Aliens</u>, Simon and Schuster.

described as terrifying, some have been viewed as pleasurable or transformative.

The first alien abduction claim to be widely publicized was the Betty and Barney Hill abduction in 1961[33]. Reports of the abduction phenomenon have been made around the world, but are most common in English speaking countries, especially the United States. The contents of the abduction narrative often seem to vary with the home culture of the alleged abductee.

It is interesting to note that memories recovered by

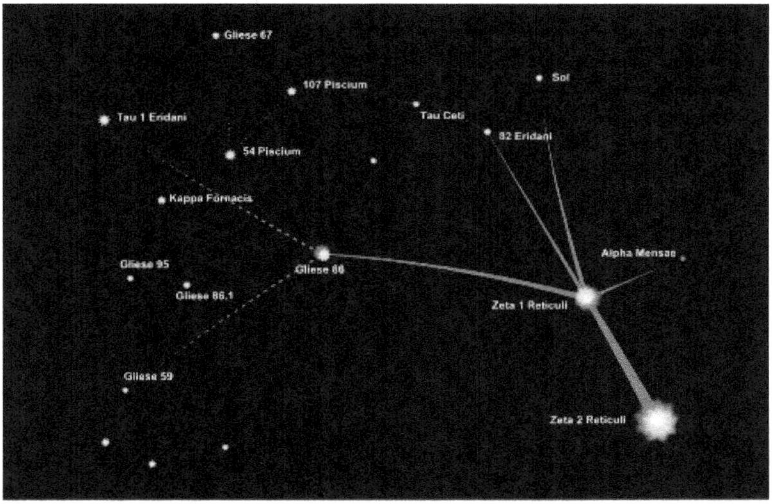

Figure 33: The star map seen by Betty Hill on board a UFO

Betty Hill under hypnosis resulted in her being able to draw a fairly accurate star map she had seen on board the craft which contained information she had no knowledge of prior to the abduction.

---

[33] Friedman, Stanton & Kathleen Marden. Captured! The Betty and Barney Hill UFO Experience. Franklin Lakes, NJ: New Page Books, 2007.

Alien abductions have been the subject of conspiracy theories and science fiction storylines (notably The X-Files) that have speculated on stealth technology required if the phenomenon were real, the motivations for secrecy, and that alien implants could be a possible form of physical evidence.

However, while there have been many modern tales of abduction, alien abductions are actually far older than most people believe. In fact they date back thousands of years and are written about in some of the oldest religious literature.

As an example, let us go to the year 850 B C, to the shores of the Jordan River in Israel where the Prophet Elijah was abducted. Of course, many would believe that calling this an abduction is blasphemy since he was taken up by God according to the Scriptures. However, boiled down to its most basic facts, a human was taken away by a power from the sky. Stripped of its religious connotations, what distinguishes this event from an abduction by aliens?

Figure 34: Baal, the Phoenician Sun God

The Prophet Elijah[34] practiced what we would call his ministry in Israel during the reigns of King Ahab[35] and his son King Abaziah[36]. The trouble began when King Ahab married the pagan princess Jezebel and she erected an altar to Baal in Samaria.

Figure 35: An Icon of Elijah

Baal was the Sun-God of the Phoenicians and a Sacred Pole was used to chart Baal's journey through the twelve signs of the zodiac. According to the Old Testament of the Holy Bible by embracing the religion of a "false god", Ahab did more to anger the Lord than any of the kings of Israel before him. It would seem that Ahab's God was very sensitive about the worship of other gods.

The Prophet known as Elijah (Elias) the Tishbite then delivered a divine message to King Ahab that God would bring a drought to his kingdom. The upshot of this message was that since Baal was worshipped for his supposed power over the sky and the weather, that God's message was a direct challenge to Baal and a sign of God's displeasure.

After Elijah's confrontation with Ahab, God tells him to flee out of Israel, to a hiding place by the brook Cherith, east of the Jordan, where he will be fed by ravens. When the

Figure 36: Elijah in the WIlderness by Allston

1 Kings 16:29 to 2Kings 2:18
[35] 874-853 B C
[36] 853-852 B C

brook dries up, God sends him to a widow living in the town of Zarephatho in Phoenicia. When Elijah finds her and asks to be fed, she says that she does not have sufficient food to keep her and her own son alive. Elijah tells her that God will not allow her supply of flour or oil to run out, saying, "*Don't be afraid..this is what the Lord, the God of Israel, says: 'The jar of flour will not be used up and the jug of oil will not run dry until the day the Lord gives rain on the land.*"

    She feeds him the last of their food, and Elijah's promise miraculously comes true; thus, by an act of faith the woman received the promised blessing. God gave her "manna" from heaven even while he was withholding food from his unfaithful people in the Promised Land. Sometime later the widow's son dies and the widow cries, "Did you come to remind me of my sin and kill my son?" Moved by a faith like that of Abraham[37], Elijah prays that God might restore her son so that the veracity and trustworthiness of God's word might be demonstrated. 1 Kings 17:22 relates how God "*heard the voice of Elijah; and the soul of the child came into him again, and he revived.*"

    This is the first instance of raising the dead recorded in Scripture. This non-Israelite widow was granted the best covenant blessing in the person of her son, the only hope for a widow in ancient society. The widow cried, "...the word of the Lord from your mouth is the truth." She made a confession that the Israelites had failed to make.

    After more than three years of drought and famine, God tells Elijah to return to Ahab and announce the end of the drought: not occasioned by repentance in Israel but by

---

[37] (Romans 4:17, Hebrews 11:19)

the command of the Lord, who had determined to reveal himself again to his people. While on his way, Elijah meets Obadiah, the head of Ahab's household, who had hidden a hundred prophets of the God of Israel when Ahab and Jezebel had been killing them. Elijah sends Obadiah back to Ahab to announce his return to Israel.

The primary evidence that Elijah was taken up comes from the Holy Bible[38]. In 2nd Kings Elijah reveals that he was about to be taken away;

> *"And it came to pass, when they were gone over, that Elijah said unto Elisha, Ask what shall I do for thee, before I be taken away from thee. And Elisha said, I pray thee, let a double portion of thy spirit be upon me. And he said though hast asked a hard thing; nevertheless, if thou see me when I am taken from thee, it shall be so unto thee, but if not, it shall not be so.*
>
> *And it came to pass, as they still went on, and talked that behold, there appeared a chariot of fire, and horses of fire, and parted them both asunder; and Elijah went up by a whirlwind into heaven[39]."*

THE ABDUCTION OF EZEKIEL

In 593 B C, in Chaldea in the country of Iraq, the Bible states that the Prophet Ezekiel saw a strange craft appear in the sky above him. *It consisted of "wheels within wheels," a brilliant dome, and four beings. He was transported to a mountain top, without knowing how he got*

---

[38] The second chapter of 2 Kings.
[39] 2 Kings, 2:11

there and remained stunned, an experience reminiscent of numerous modern reports by people claiming to have been abducted by aliens.

The account of Ezekiel's contact with unknown forces was actually written down centuries after the life of the prophet and so it does not represent a first-hand report of an observation. However, it is interesting to note that Ezekiel struggled to describe something that was beyond his frame of reference.

THE ABDUCTION OF ENOCH

Enoch appears in the Book of Genesis and a figure in the Generations of Adam. Enoch is the son of Jared[40], the father of Methuselah, and the great-grandfather of Noah. The text reads—uniquely in the Generations—that Enoch *"walked with God: and he was no more; for God took him*[41]*"*. While this abduction is wrapped up in religious fervor and religious text, it is clear that Enoch, a human was taken away

Figure 37: Enoch the Patriarch by Gerard Hoet

---

[40] Genesis 5:3-18
[41] Genesis 5:22-29

by what was referred to as "God." The only thing that makes the taking of Enoch different than the taking of any modern abductee is the belief that Enoch was taken by God. How does this materially differ from being taken by an alien?

OTHER ABDUCTIONS AND VISITATIONS

Of course it was not just the Bible Prophets of the Old Testament who had intercourse with God or the "gods." Common folks did as well.

In March of the year 260 a strange incident happened in China. At a time when the government of Wu faced a number of dangers, during the reign of Sun Hsiu[42] the generals that commanded the border garrisons used to leave their wives and children[43] as pledges of their loyalty to the government. It was not unusual for a dozen or so of these children to play together at any given time.

According to Chinese records, a strange child suddenly joined the hostage children in their play. He was described as being less than four feet tall, dressed in dark clothes, and appeared to be between six and seven years old. None of the other children recognized the newcomer, so what family he belonged to that he should suddenly appear among them?

His reply was that he came to join them only because they seemed to be enjoying themselves so much. On closer examination it was noticed that light rays from the little boy's eyes flashed brilliantly, and the other children began to be afraid. At this point he asked, "*Do you*

---

[42] 258-263
[43] These children came to be known as hostage children.

fear me then? Don't. Though I am not human, I am the star-god Yung-huo (Mars) and have come to deliver a message to you" 'The Three Lords will return to Ssu-ma.'"

The children were startled and some ran off to tell their parents. The adults arrived in haste to witness all this, but the visitor said, *"I must leave you."* So saying, he propelled his body upward and transformed himself.

Since there was an ongoing political crisis, no one reported what the star-god said however, four years later Hsiu was overthrown and 21 years later Wu was overthrown and the power fell to Ssu-ma[44]. What this prophetic little boy a god, an alien or both. Certainly his prophecy came to pass so what was he, he could change form and he could levitate and make prophecies. Was he a god in the true sense of the word or something else?

In 428 in Constantinople in the country of Turkey a child was abducted and supposedly taken to Heaven. The scene was one of total chaos as an earthquake had just destroyed the ancient city of Constantinople. This massive quake had leveled the massive walls and the fifty-seven towers. Just as the people were starting to shake off their shock there came a new tremor even stronger than those previously.

Nicephorus, the historian, reported that in their fright, the inhabitants of Byzantium (one of the early names for Constantinople) abandoned the city and gathered in the countryside. They were praying that the city be spared total

---

[44] *In the Wu Kingdom during the Three Kingdoms Period (222-280)* cited in the In Search for the Supernatural: The Written Record, trans. Kenneth J. DeWoskin and J. I. Crump (Stanford University Press, 1996.)

destruction. Suddenly a miracle happened that filled everyone with admiration.

"In the midst of the entire crowd, a child was suddenly taken up by a strong force, so high into the air that they lost sight of him. After this he came down as he had gone up, and told Patriarch Proclus, the Emperor himself, and the assembled multitude that he had just attended a great concert of the Angels hailing the Lord in their sacred canticles[45]."

Such was the amazement of the crowd that they regained their courage and when the tremors had stopped returned to rebuild their city. A "convenient" miracle I would say which served to strengthen the religion of the people as well as assure the rebuilding of what became a very important city.

In the year 760 in France during the reign of Pepin the Short (715-768) there were reports of a large number of extraordinary phenomena seen in the skies of France. There were numerous sightings of human figures, ships with sails and battling armies. Additionally, several individuals reported that they had been abducted by aerial beings[46].

And finally, in the year 999 in the Abbey of Saint-Leger, Cote d'Or, France there was a very mysterious bedroom visitation. Rodulphus Glaber[47], a monk and a writer, reported that "Not so long ago such (visions)

---

[45] From the chronicler Nicephorus Callistus (14th century) also in a letter by Acacius, Patriarch of Constantinople (died in 489) to Peter Fullo, Patriarch of Antioch, also in a letter by Pope Felix III (483-492) to Peter Fullo.

[46] Garinet, Jules, *Histoire de la Magie en France* (Paris 1818)

[47] Rudolphi, *Glabri, Historiarum Libri Quinque ab anno incarnationis DCCC usque ad annum MXLIV*, Book V, Chapter 1.

happened to me, by the favor of God. At the time I was staying in the monastery of the martyr Saint-Leger, also named *Abbaye de Champeaux*. I saw one night, before Matines, a hideous little monster of vaguely human form appear at the foot of my bed. It seemed to be as much as I could discern, of medium size with a frail neck, a thin face, very black eyes, a wrinkled and narrow forehead, a goatee, straight and pointed ears, straight and dirty hair, dog teeth, a sharp occiput, its breast swollen, a bump on the back, hanging buttocks and dirty clothes, with its whole body appearing to shake.

Unfortunately, Glaber viewed this appearance in religious terms and ran to the altar to confess his sins. Someone not predisposed to seeing everything as a sign from God might have had a more rational approach to this bedroom invasion.

Clearly, there have been many more abductions and visitations than have ever been revealed. The UFO abduction reports of today are nothing new; these "aliens" have clearly manipulated and guided mankind for eons. The question is why?

CHAPTER SEVEN

ANOMOLOUS CITIES AND TECHNOLOGY

Science believes that we know everything about everything and if something does not fit into their

Figure 38: Model of a swept-wing aircraft found in an ancient tomb

preconceived ideas then it must be a fake. This attitude has done much to hide the true history of this planet and our civilization.

There have been many items found in ancient cities that show that our history is not what science says it has to be. There are even entire civilizations that seem to have been dropped in the locations where they flourished.

As an example of the blind eye that science turns to what they cannot explain, consider the following.

If science wasn't so sure that dinosaurs and man missed each other by approximately 40 million years, they might have described one of the figurines discussed in the following article as a dinosaur rather than a dragon. Of course, Christians believe that "dinosaurs" were created in the same week as man. Christians thus shouldn't be surprised when evidence that dinosaurs and man co-existed.

This story came from the Sofia News Agency, July 10, 2007

Bulgarian archaeologists have found two unique ceramic figurines of a cobra and dragon heads as they continue excavation at the rock sanctuary of Perperikon, near Kardzhali in southern Bulgaria.

The two figurines were part of the ornaments of a clay altar dating roughly to the period between the 3rd and 1st centuries before Christ, said archaeologist Nikolai Ovcharov, who oversees the dig.

The finds are probably part of the Tsepina culture, named after one of the key Thracian fortresses in the Rodopi Mountains, which played an important strategic role well into the medieval era.

The two finds are more important than the Roman era finds because they offer much more insight into the distinctive traits of the local culture, Ovcharov said.

Snakes were considered guardians of the deeps and, as such, were closely associated to the cult of Dionysus, whose shrine the Bulgarian archaeologists are currently excavating.

The next stage of the dig, which is staffed by close to 150 people, is to examine the southern quarter of the city, where the archaeologists hope to remain the remains of a third palace, dating back to the Thracian era.

The city of Perperikon has been inhabited since around 5000 BC, while a nearby shrine dedicated to Orpheus, near the village of Tatul, dates back to 6000 BC and is older than the Pyramids of Giza.

THE MYSTERIOUS OLMECS

3000+ Year Old Giant head found buried 20 ft. deep with the use of magnetic mapping. What was an Advanced, Black, or possibly Asian or East Indian) non-Egyptian, pre-Hispanic civilization doing in Mexico--in the America's prior to and more advanced than the Maya and the Aztecs?

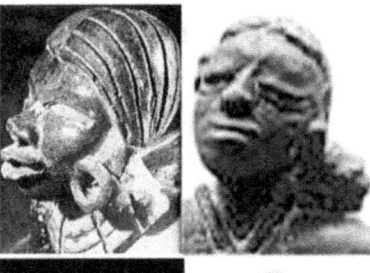

No one knows for certain where they came from, where they went or how they moved those huge stone sculptures from distant quarries. Traditional archeology doesn't have the answers--but if you believe that man has always been advanced you can see

where they may have come from.

Readers of my books, and especially of The Lost Realms, as well as of a previous article on this website titled "The Case of the Missing Elephant," know by now that beginning with the discovery of a colossal stone head in 1869, an advanced civilization that preceded the Mayas and Aztecs of Mexico came to light.

Its leaders and bearers were unmistakably black Africans. They were arbitrarily named by archaeologists "Olmecs"; and their embarrassing enigma -- of who they were, and how they had come across the ocean, and why, was compounded by the timing of their arrival in the New World.

Once it was conceded (very grudgingly!) that the 'Olmecs' did indeed represent the earliest or even Mother Civilization of Mesoamerica, the date of their arrival was at first set at about 250 B.C.; then at about 500 B.C.; then farther back and back, until 1500 B.C. was acknowledged.

But I have argued for a date twice as old! 3000 years is now accepted..." Sitchin

In a prior article, we examined the "mysterious" Olmecs, a people who preceded the Hispanic civilizations in South and Central America such as the Mayas and the Incas and yet were more advanced.

Mysterious because no one knows who they were or where they came from. Their artifacts indicate that they were either African, Asian or Hindu.

According to orthodox archaeology, none of those people should have been there or even had the wherewithal to get there. Columbus discovered the Americas, right?

We thought that these pieces were of interest because of their apparent similarities; though they are from ancient Pakistan/India and/or Mexico, with distinct and perhaps exaggerated "African" ☐ features.

The dancing girl from the Indus Valley is itself a product of a mysterious, multi-ethnic civilization. Will Hart and Robert Berringer write:

"¦....We should wonder how an ancient culture of which nothing is known, not even their language, created this sophisticated city at a point in time many thousands of years ahead of the curve? Civil engineers do not crawl out of thatched-roof huts able to draw up plans for a complex urban environment." ☐

What's true about the Olmec's? We don't know. What we do know is whatever you've read in the conventional paradigm affirming textbooks is incorrect.

MAN AND DINOSAUR TOGETHER

"I visited the Three Rivers Pertoglyph site this spring, but didn't have time to scrutinize the whole of it, so when I found someone had posted their pictures I took the time to peruse them.

They had one labled: "Impossible, but It sure looks to me like someone is hunting a dinosaur with a flaming club!" ...and it does!!!! Wish I had found it! "

There are over 21,000 petroglyphs at the Three Rivers Petroglyph Site at Three Rivers, New Mexico located midway between Tularosa and Carrizozo in Otero County on highway 54. Many of the petroglyphs can be easily viewed from a trail open to the public which winds through the rocks for about one mile. The petroglyphs are thought to be the product of the Jornada Mogollon people between about 1000 and 1400 AD. The site is protected and maintained by the Bureau of Land Management.

The petroglyphs at Three Rivers were recorded during a 6 year project by the Archaeological Society of New Mexico's Rock Art Recording Field Schools. Photographs and records are on file at the Bureau of Land Management's District Office in Las Cruces....Wikipedia

Here is the original site where a larger photo of the petroglyph --along with others--can be found

CHINESE DINOSAURS

Previously, here, we noted the close similarity of the Ishtar Gate "Dragon", (604-562 BC) to images of similar creatures from the Egyptians (2600 B.C. and older), the Han Dynasty (206 B.C. to 220 A.D.) as well as Tang Dynasty (618-906 A.D.) the Sung Dynasty (1127-1279A.D) and possibly others.

This was evidence that the creature was real and not mythological. The representations of the creature were consistent across time and geographical location. We had even offered some suggestions concerning its identification based on fossil dinosaur re-creations.

The drawing above is of a Han Dynasty Motif showing a man hunting this Egypto/Assyrian/Chinese dragon with what appears to be a sling or a bolo weapon. Further evidence, we believe that this was in fact a real creature.

THE MYSTERIOUS BLACK KNIGHT

If aliens created the human race as some believe it would seem logical that the aliens would leave some way to monitor their creation. Impossible you say, but perhaps not.

There are around 3000 human-made satellites in working order around the Earth, however if the debris of old and damaged satellites are taken into account the number increases dramatically. Ever since the Soviet Union launched the very first artificial satellite into orbit in 1957, various countries around the world have sought to compete and satellites today are used for communication, navigation and exploration. It would seem that there is nothing mysterious about these scientific marvels. However, these satellites are relatively unexciting in comparison to the mystery surrounding one very old dark satellite.

Legend has it that in orbit around the Earth is a mysterious, dark object which dates back perhaps 13 000 years. Its origin and purpose are inscrutable, dubbed the "Black Knight" this elusive satellite has allegedly been beaming signals towards the Earth and inspected by NASA astronauts yet only a few on Earth officially know of its existence. The origin of the ominous name is part of the enigma; it is impossible to discover who first called it this or indeed why. Humans have only in the last 60 years had the technology to launch a man-made object into space so what is the logical explanation of tales of an alien intruder on our doorstep?

Figure 40: Is there a alien satellite in polar orbit?

The first apparent part of this story begins with signals heard by Nikola Tesla (1856-1943) a brilliant Serbian inventor (and possibly a genuine mad scientist) who spent most of his career in the USA. He was an electrical engineer and produced works which explored the idea of radio and wireless transmissions. In 1899, he reportedly intercepted a signal unlike any of the natural sources from Earth such as electrical storms that he had already investigated in his experiments. Instead he announced that regular signals must from an intelligent outside source, potentially inhabitants of Mars. Today there are those who say he was listening to a transmission from an orbiting satellite of unknown origin later called by some the Black Knight.

It is more likely that what was Tesla detected was not the Black Knight but instead signals which are emitted from natural objects. Today we know of natural extraterrestrial sources such as pulsars. These are fast-spinning neutron stars which emit a rhythmic signal. They were first discovered in 1967 by Northern Irish astrophysicist Jocelyn Bell-Burnell (1943-). Until certain of their origin, they were jokingly nicknamed the Little Green Men signals. Tesla was likely completely unaware of what he really detected (if indeed he picked up anything at all).

In the 1920s anomalous signals were again detected by amateur radio operators. These were originally of Earthly origin, but their timing was bizarre! A signal would be received then a second repeated signal received a few seconds later. These Long Delayed Echoes (LDEs) were difficult to explain in terms or radio waves bouncing off atmospheric layers. In 1973, Scotsman Duncan Lunan

(1945-) went back to these signals to see if could make sense of them. Miraculously by plotting the delay times against the order in which the echoes were received he could create what appeared to be star charts and diagrams. By deciphering them Lunan decided that the signals were actually messages transmitted by a probe originally from the star Epsilon Böotes (Izar) which had been lurking near the Moon for the past 13 000 years. Lunan is not a professional astronomer but instead a science fiction author with a flair for outré ideas but nevertheless the name Black Knight is never mentioned by him; nor has he personally linked his Epsilon Böotes hypothesis with the Black Knight, others seem to be responsible for this. (UPDATE: Mr. Lunan has stated his position on the Black Knight story in the Comments section below.)

Another story dating back to the early 1950s claimed to refer to an apparition of the Black Knight reports the detection of a signal of by an object in orbit. This was a time of deep suspicions held by the two superpowers on either side of the Pacific. Neither the Americans nor the Soviets had the ability to place an object into any kind of an orbit at that time. Yet the discovery of an Earth-orbiting satellite was reported in a couple of newspapers from the time, and the respected astronomer Clyde Tombaugh (discoverer of Pluto) is said to have been involved. However, the articles actually a couple of synopses of a book by the Ufological author Donald Keyhoe (1897-1988). I'm sure these promotional newspaper articles had been great for sales of the book!

A few years later, the Black Knight seemed have made another appearance when American newspapers reported in 1960 that there was an unusual object in polar orbit, by then both superpowers had satellites in equatorial orbit but polar orbit meant that the satellite could see every part of the Earth, yet neither country admitted owning it. This may seem strange but remember that this was a time of deep-rooted suspicion and espionage not just with each other but now seemingly with extra-terrestrials too. Declassified information now released from that time suggested that object was a Corona spy satellite under disguise at the time of the US Discoverer research satellite program. The world was bracing itself for nuclear destruction, coming close to a nuclear war in the Cuban Missile Crisis just two years later, had this information been released at the time perhaps the Cold War would have indeed heated up.

The most recent and most cited "evidence" for a mystery satellite from beyond dates from 1998. The crew of Space Shuttle Orbiter Endeavour photographed an unusual object in low Earth orbit. These images are often labelled as the most definite proof of this satellite.

CHAPTER EIGHT

SIGNS OF LIFE ON THE MOON

Figure 41: The Moon

Our Moon roughly 239,000 miles away and roughly the size of the USA around 2000 miles in diameter and is still one of the biggest mysteries of all time. We are told that the Moon is a dead world, probably scooped out of the area that became the Pacific Ocean. Prepare to be shocked as we show you that most of what you think you know about our satellite is not true.

The Moon is the only natural satellite of the Earth and the fifth largest moon in the Solar System. It is the largest natural satellite of a planet in the Solar System relative to the size of its primary, having 27% the diameter and 60% the density of Earth, resulting in 1/81 (1.23%) its mass. Among satellites with known densities, the Moon is the second densest, after Io, a satellite of Jupiter.

Anybody can view the Moon in their telescope and anybody can occasionally spot anomalies of unknown origin. The Moon's orbit is such that one side faces the Earth all of the time. Nobody knows what's on the dark side of the moon but if the lighter side of the moon has buildings, cities, structures then it's quite probable that the dark side contains the same thing.

What got me into studying the moon as a kid were stories about lights and movement being seen on a supposedly dead world. When I was first starting out as a writer for a magazine, someone brought me a number for a particular photo that could be ordered from NASA. The date of the photo was during a period that no one was on the moon, but the photo showed a tracked vehicle driving across one of the craters. This was certainly an interesting image to come from a dead world.

There is a lot of speculation that the moon landings were faked because it was a way to end the cold war between the countries and show U.S. dominance over space. However, at this point, I want to cover a few issues about the moon itself.

- Where did it come from?

- Why are there so many craters?

- What are these structures that seem to show up in photos taken on the Moon?

First of all some say the moon came from earth. It was believed to have been a part of the Earth and was ripped away from this planet by a supposed strike by an asteroid. I find this hard to believe since the Moon is spherical in shape and not shaped like an asteroid space rock. Additionally a strike so massive as to scoop out something the size of the Moon should have destroyed the planet.

We are discovering that many planets have moons, some so large that they are almost like worlds of their own. My theory is that our moon was not always located near the earth but actually came from elsewhere in the galaxy. I believe our moon may have been bombarded somewhere else in our galaxy and traveled through space for perhaps millions of years until it got caught in the earth's gravitational field.

Many others believe that the Moon may be a massive space craft of some kind in disguise. It would certainly explain where all of the UFOs came from and why they appeared over this planet for thousands of years. Can you imagine any better base for a species of aliens? Millions of them could live underground or on the surface of the Moon without fear of being discovered by the primitive humans on Earth. Additionally, it is very possible that these aliens could also have established themselves on Mars as we shall see in the next chapter. These alien beings could have established bases on both Mars as well as the Moon.

The moon has a great influence on this planet. The gravitational forces of the Moon changes the tides, lights up the night skies and even is said to change our moods. There is even the so called Man in the Moon that we have all seen. Of course, we know, or should know that the features of the Man in the Moon are formed by the man craters that cover the near side of this allegedly dead world. These craters are formed as a result of the lack of atmosphere which serves to protect the Earth from the numerous bombardments of meteors that have slammed into the Moon.

Another possibility for its many craters is that they may have been built by the inhabitants of the Moon. The apparent structures on the moon that look like buildings, ships, cities, canals or things of that sort, some of them exist in the craters themselves. This one fact points to the craters (or some of them) either being fake or the structures were built after the craters were formed.

Logically, the Moon would make a very good long term base for visiting aliens. If aliens did use the Moon as a base, then there should be many more structures to be found, perhaps in that area we call the dark side of the moon. Ask yourself this why do we never go back to the after those first few publicized mission. Could it be because of the fact that we discovered that there was a race living on the Moon? We spent billions of dollars on the space program to go to the moon, so why abandon a successful program?

THE SPACESHIP MOON THEORY

The Spaceship Moon Theory, also known as the Vasin-Shcherbakov Theory, is a hypothesis that claims the Earth's moon may actually be an alien spacecraft. The hypothesis was put forth by two members of the then

Soviet Academy of Sciences, Michael Vasin and Alexander Shcherbakov, in a July 1970 article entitled "*Is the Moon the Creation of Alien Intelligence*[48]?"

Vasin and Shcherbakov's thesis was that the Moon is a hollowed-out planetoid created by unknown beings with technology far superior to any on Earth. Huge machines would have been used to melt rock and form large cavities within the Moon, with the resulting molten lava spewing out onto the Moon's surface. The Moon would therefore consist of a hull-like inner shell and an outer shell made from metallic rocky slag. For reasons unknown, the "Spaceship Moon" was then placed into orbit around the Earth.

Their hypothesis relies heavily on the suggestion that large lunar craters, generally assumed to be formed from meteor impact, are generally too shallow and have flat or even convex bottoms. Small craters have a depth proportional to their diameter but larger craters are not deeper. It is hypothesized that small meteors are making a cup-shaped depression in the rocky surface of the moon while the larger meteors are drilling through a five mile thick rocky layer and hitting a high-tensile "hull" underneath.

Additionally the authors note that the surface material of the moon is substantially composed of different elements (chromium, titanium and zirconium) from the surface of the Earth. They also note that some moon rocks are older than the oldest rocks on Earth.

---

[48] Vasin, Mikhail; Alexander Shcherbakov (July 1970). "Is The Moon The Creation of Intelligence?". Sputnik (Novosti).

They postulate that the moon comprises a rocky outer layer a few miles thick covering a strong hull perhaps 20 miles thick and beneath that there is a void, possibly containing an atmosphere. The Soviet scientists put forward the belief that the moon is not a completely natural world but a planetoid, hollowed out eons ago in the far reaches of space. Huge machines would have been used to melt rock and form large cavities within the moon, spewing the molten refuse onto the surface. Protected by a hull-like inner shell plus a reconstructed outer shell of metallic rocky junk, this gigantic craft, they believed, was steered through the cosmos and finally parked in orbit around our earth.

The theory was re-vitalized in 1975 with the publication of *Our Mysterious Spaceship Moon* by Don Wilson[49]. He stated that,

"Too many pieces of evidence seem to fit to reject the theory without investigation."

There is even tantalizing evidence that in the dim recesses of human memory there have been recollections of a time before the arrival of the moon. Aristotle told of a people who lived in Arcadia, a mountainous region in Central Greece, long before the coming of the Greeks. The Greek term Proscelene means before the moon. In Tibetan texts there are stories of a people on a lost continent called Gondwana, said to be civilized before the moon shone in the night sky.

Bolivian symbols have been interpreted by Dr. P. Allen as records that a satellite came into orbit around the Earth about 11,500 to 13,000 years ago.

---

[49] Wilson, Don W. (1975). Our Mysterious Spaceship Moon (1st ed.). New York: Dell.

SECRETS OF THE SPACE PROGRAM

As was mentioned early, the U.S. spent billions of dollars to fund what was called a civilian space program. The National Aeronautics and Space Administration (NASA) is the agency of the United States government that is responsible for the nation's civilian space program and for aeronautics and aerospace research.

President Dwight D. Eisenhower established the National Aeronautics and Space Administration (NASA) in 1958[5] with a distinctly civilian (rather than military) orientation encouraging peaceful applications in space science. The National Aeronautics and Space Act was passed on July 29, 1958, disestablishing NASA's predecessor, the National Advisory Committee for Aeronautics (NACA). The new agency became operational on October 1, 1958.

Since that time, most U.S. space exploration efforts have been led by NASA, including the Apollo moon-landing missions, the Skylab space station, and later the Space Shuttle. Currently, NASA is supporting the International Space Station and is overseeing the development of the Orion Multi-Purpose Crew Vehicle, the Space Launch System and Commercial Crew vehicles. The agency is also responsible for the Launch Services Program (LSP) which provides oversight of launch operations and countdown management for unmanned NASA launches.

NASA science is focused on better understanding Earth through the Earth Observing System, advancing heliophysics through the efforts of the Science Mission Directorate's Heliophysics Research Program, exploring bodies throughout the Solar System with advanced robotic missions such as New Horizons, and researching astrophysics topics, such as the Big Bang, through the Great Observatories and associated programs. NASA shares data with various national and international organizations such as from the Greenhouse Gases Observing Satellite.

Of course, what few knew was that the National Aeronautical and Space Administration (NASA) was based in part on Nazi technology and was run for some time by a former Nazi[50]. What was kept even more secret was that NASA was actually under the Department of Defense, so much for the civilian space program.

At the time the space program started, the American people were told that we knew very little about the Moon. However, it has now come to light this this was not exactly true. To get more of the real story you must go to Moffett Field.

Moffett Federal Airfield (IATA: NUQ, ICAO: KNUQ, FAA LID: NUQ), also known as Moffett Field, is a joint civil-military airport located between northern Mountain View and northern Sunnyvale, California, USA[51].

The airport is near the south end of San Francisco Bay, northwest of San Jose. Formerly a United States Navy facility, the former naval air station is now owned and operated by the NASA Ames Research Center. Tenant military activities include the 129th Rescue Wing of the California Air National Guard, operating the MC-130P Combat Shadow and HH-60G Pave Hawk aircraft, as well

---

[50] Dr. Werner Von Braun had headed Hitler's V2 Program.
[51] http://en.wikipedia.org/wiki/Moffett_Federal_Airfield

Evidence of Alien Contact 109

as the adjacent Headquarters for the 7th Psychological Operations Group of the U.S. Army Reserve. Until 28 July 2010, the U.S. Air Force's 21st Space Operations Squadron was also a tenant command at Moffett Field, occupying the former Onizuka Air Force Station. In addition to these military activities, NASA also operates several of its own aircraft from Moffett.

At this former military installation is a

Figure 42: Some of the 48,000 pounds of lunar film

MacDonald's Restaurant that closed in 2008. Behind the counter of this abandoned McDonalds lie 48,000 lbs. of 70mm tape the only copy of extremely high-resolution images of the moon[52].

These tapes were recorded 40 years ago as part of the Apollo program to map the lunar surface to plan landing spots for Apollo 11 onward. They have never been seen by the public because at the time, they were classified

---

52

as they reveal the extreme precision of our spy satellites. Instead, all we have ever seen are the grainy photo-of-a-photo images that were released to the public.

The spacecraft did not ship this film back to Earth. Instead, they developed the film on the Lunar Orbiter and then raster scanned the negatives with a 5 micron spot (200 lines/millimeter resolution) and beamed the data back to Earth using yet-to-be-patented-by-others lossless analog compression. Three ground stations on Earth (one was in Madrid) recorded the transmissions on these magnetic tapes.

The sharpness of this old film makes it very clear that the U.S. Government should be well aware of any structures and/or installations on the moon. So why haven't we been told? So now the questions are why these unique films hidden in a closed McDonalds and why weren't the American people made aware of these films?

WHERE DID THE MOON ORIGINATE?

As there is very little similarity between the makeup of the moon and earth, the old theory that the moon broke off our planet and ended up in its orbit can be discounted.

It therefore appears that the moon originated in another part of the universe before moving into the earth's orbit. However, author and science expert, Isaac Asimov believed that the moon was too large to have been captured by our orbit. The orbit of the moon itself is also enigmatic. It orbit is a perfect circle and stationary, with only one side being exposed to earth. As far as we know, the moon is the only natural satellite with such an orbit.

Author and expert on the ancient Sumerian civilization, Zecharia Sitchin also had an interest in the moon. Our mysterious satellite has caused much argument among scientists with respect to its age and origin. Sitchin wrote in his book *Genesis Revisited* (1990), some answers are provided if we go back to the Sumerian cosmology. The assertion here is that the moon originated not as a satellite of Earth but the much larger planet, Tiamat, which originally orbited beyond Mars.

The Sumerian cosmology describes an unstable solar system caused by emerging gravitational forces disturbing planetary balance and causing moons to grow disproportionately. According to the Sumerians, one of the eleven moons of Tiamat grew to an unusual size and proved to be increasingly disruptive to the other planets. It was named 'Kingu'.

In an ensuing celestial battle, Tiamat was split in two; one half was shattered; the other half, accompanied by Kingu, was thrust into a new orbit to become the Earth and its moon.

LUNAR ECLIPSES

Another interesting question regarding the Earth/Moon relationship concerns the lunar eclipse. Why is it that the moon is just the right distance from the earth to completely cover the sun during an eclipse?

Figure 43: A lunar eclipse

While the diameter of the moon is a mere 2,160 miles against the sun's gigantic 864,000 miles, it is never the less in just the proper position to block out the sun's corona when it moves between the sun and earth. Isaac Asimov explains, "*there is no reason why the moon and the sun should fit so well.*"

It is the sheerest of coincidences, and only the Earth is among all the planets blessed in this fashion. Rather than a fluke of nature, it seems more like it could have been done intentionally.

IS THE MOON OLDER THAN THE EARTH AND THE SUN?

It is believed that the moon could possibly be older than the earth and sun. Scientists have dated some moon rocks as billions of years old. Some have been dated back as far as 4.5 billion years.

Scientists nowadays accept the moon to be 4.6 billion years old.

Harvard's respected astronomy journal, *Sky and Telescope*, reported that at a lunar conference in 1973 dated a lunar rock as 5.3 billion years old which would make it almost a billion years older than our planet.

ARE THE ROCKS FROM THE MOON UNIQUE?

Scientists found that the crushed up rocks on the moon is of another world.

Analysis has shown that the moon rocks are of a completely different composition to the soil around them. Some of the rocks gathered by a Soviet mission in 1970 were resistant to rusting. This is not a feature of any metal known to man and years ahead of our technology though there have been a few metal objects made of such metal in antiquity. The moon has three distinct layers of rocks. Contrary to the idea heavier rocks sink, the heavier rocks are found on the surface.

According to Don Wilson *"The abundance of titanium and other refractory elements in the surface areas is so pronounced that several geo-chemists proposed that refractory compounds were bought to the moon's surface in great quantity in some unknown way. That this was done cannot be questioned. These materials which are usually concentrated towards the interior of a world are now on the outside."*

Earl Ubel, who was a former science director for CBS Television added to the mystery by stating that, *"The first layer (20 miles deep), consists of lava-like material similar to lava flows on Earth. The second, extending down to 50 miles, is made up of somewhat denser rock. The third, continuing to a depth of at least 80 miles and probably below, appears to be of a heavier metal, similar to the Earth's mantle."*

Many of the rock samples discovered on the moon have also been found to be magnetized. It has been suggested that this is due to their exposure to the magnetism present on earth.

Others have rebutted this claim by arguing that if such an influence was placed on the moon, the earth's magnetism would have caused the destruction of the moon and its orbit many millions of years ago. Huge disk shaped objects located beneath the moons lava seas!

The moon has large seas of smooth molten rock. Known as 'maria', four fifths of these are on the Earth-side hemisphere. In the center of these marias huge disk-shaped objects have been detected lying 20 to 40 miles below the surface.

The objects are referred to as 'mascons' and they are said to be located like a bulls-eye at the center of the marias. The mascons were first discovered because their density distorted the orbits of objects flying over or near them.

Some scientists have theorized that the mascons are heavy iron ore meteorites that plunged into the moon when it was in a soft and formable state.

IS THERE VOLCANIC ACTION ON THE MOON?

In 1963 astronomers at the Lowell Observatory saw a reddish glow on the crests of the ridges in the Aristarchus region.

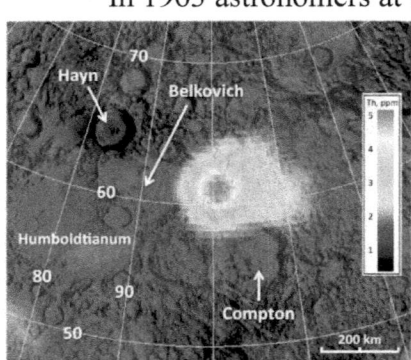

Figure 44: Signs of active volcano on the dark side of the moon

This was after a similar glow and gaseous explosions were photographed by Russian astronomer Nikolay A. Kozyrev in 1958. Other observatories also reported red glow. Although the moon is deemed to be volcanically dead it seems that there is certainly something creaking in its interior.

Seismographic equipment left at six separate sites on the moon by the Apollo missions picked up a great deal of activity until it ceased operating in 1977.

OPERATION MOONBLINK

In the early nineteenth century, Sir John Herschel in England saw unidentified lights on the moon during an eclipse and noted that some of the lights appeared to be moving above the moon.

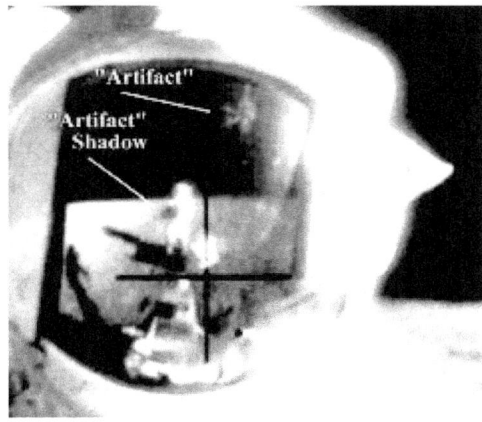

Figure 45: Reflection shows an anamoloy

Other astronomers of the period also reported seeing a geometrical pattern of lights that resembled city streets. In the mid 1960's NASA established the operation to investigate many strange flashes of light over the moon. The space association had received reports of many extraordinary lunar events.

In 1959 a dark object had been observed hovering over the moon for two hours. On July 29, John O'Neill observed a nineteen kilometer long bridge straddling the crater Mare Crisium. One month later famous British astronomer Dr H. Wilkins verified the sighting.

Project Moon-Blink was a draft NASA created in 1965-1966, for the exploration of unusual phenomena (anomalies) on the surface of the Moon. Work performed by Trident Engineering Associates (Annapolis, Maryland) under contract NAS 5-9613 dated June 1, 1965, Goddard Space Flight Center (Grinbelt, Maryland). In the twelve months to September 1966, Operation Moonblink had detected 28 unusual lunar events.

In a report issued by NASA in October 1966, the background is described as follows:

There have been some puzzling reports over the years. Before 1843 astronomers listed Linne as a normal but steep-walled crater about five miles in diameter. In 1866 Schmidt, a famed astronomer reported that Linne was not a crater at all but looked more like a whitish cloud. Later observers disagreed with both descriptions, saying it was a low mound" about four miles across, with a deep crater one mile in diameter in its top.

Much later — in 1961 — Patrick Moore, one of the foremost contemporary lunar astronomers, was astonished that Linne appeared to be a normal crater about three miles in diameter. Moore examined it with two telescopes then called another astronomer. He examined it with a third instrument and reported a similar inexplicable appearance. The following night was cloudy, but the next night Linne appeared as Moore had always seen it — a gently rounded dome with a small crater on top. Moore attributed the changes to unusual lighting effects. During the past ten years several incontrovertible observations have been reported of unusual color activity on or just above the lunar surface. These may be divided into two categories: those events localized to a few square miles of lunar area and those covering a significant portion of the lunar surface. Insufficient evidence exists at present to determine whether these two types of events are similar or dissimilar in nature. However, they both manifest themselves in the red portion of the visible spectrum. The localized observations to date have occurred most frequently in two lunar areas: the Aristarchus region and Alphonsus. Appendix I of this report lists a number of modern observations which are peculiar because of color changes. Most were of short duration — minutes or hours. The detection of these transient events demands a program of constant surveillance of the moon with suitable astronomical instruments. This was strongly recommended by Dr. Z. Kopal at Commission 17 (The Moon) sponsored by the IAU and NASA at Goddard Space Flight Center on April 15–16, 1965. A surveillance program utilizing large astronomical telescopes inherently capable of detecting these occurrences is not feasible because of problems caused by economics and/or by prior commitments. In 1968 an obelisk shaped object was discovered. This became known as the 'Shard'. The object rose nearly two and a half kilometers above the Urkert area of the moon's surface, which rises more than eight kilometers from the Sinus Medii region. No known natural process can explain the structure.

A HOLLOW MOON

There are many indications that the moon is hollow.

Figure 46: Is the Moon hollow?

The moon's mean density- about 3.34 grams per cubic centimeter is significantly less than the 5.5 gram density of the earth's mantle. This density indicates that the moon may not have a core.

The most starling evidence came on November 20 1969, when the Apollo 12 crew, after returning to their command ship, sent the lunar module ascent stage crashing down back on to the moon, creating an artificial earthquake. The crash site was 40 miles from where the astronauts had left their seismic devices. The ultra-sensitive equipment recorded the moon ringing like a bell for more almost forty minutes. The vibration took almost eight minutes to reach a peak and then diminished in intensity.

This ringing was repeated when the Apollo 13's third stage fell to the lunar surface, striking with the equivalent of eleven tons of TNT. According to NASA, this time the moon reacted like a gong.

Although seismic equipment was 108 miles from the crash site, recordings showed reverberations lasted for three hours and twenty minutes and traveled to a depth of twenty-two to twenty-five miles. Subsequent studies of man-made crashes yielded similar results. After one impact the moon reverberated for four hours.

On March 13, 1972, a large meteorite struck the moon with the equivalent of 200 ton of TNT. After sending shockwaves deep into the interior of the moon, scientists were baffled to find that none returned, revealing that there was something unusual about the moon's core.

It seems the moon has a tough outer shell but a light or non-existent interior. This would certainly fit the description of a hollow moon with a very tough exterior.

CHAPTER NINE

ARE ALIENS ON THE MOON?

LUNA LIFE

The Moon is far from being an inert and lifeless world. Many centuries of observation have noted occurrences on the lunar surface which take the form of glows, mists, flashes and similar illuminations. They have become more popularly described as Lunar Transient Phenomena (LTP), thanks to noted astronomer Patrick Moore who coined the phrase. It largely encompasses all such recorded signs of activity now generally thought to be volcanic in nature.

Ancient peoples throughout the world held the moon and its periodic eclipses in awe and for many it was a source of worship. From this sprang numerous intriguing myths and legends, including the notion firmly held by many Greeks that this small neighbor of Earth's was inhabited also. Lucian of Samosata, although Syrian, was a widely regarded Greek satirist and lyracist.

He first wrote of his travels to that "great country in the air" in a published work entitled: 'True History'.

Although more fiction that fact, it told the tale of a voyage in a sailing ship carried aloft by a whirlwind to the moon and a subsequent meeting with its inhabitants; claimed to be much like those of Earth.

In 1516 Lodovico Ariosto wrote an epic poem in which the theme was a lunar trip by way of "firie chariet". The astronomer Johannes Kepler, who published his famous 'Laws of Planetary Motion' between 1609 and 1618, also wrote 'Dream'; a book full of fantasies and visions based on the science of the day that included the idea of moon-dwellers. It was in the same year, 1634, that Lucian of Samosata's original work was first published in England.

Now the idea of life on other worlds was beginning to form in earnest and Bishop Francis Godwin pursued this theme four years later when he wrote: 'The Man in the Moon'. It recorded the adventures of a fictitious Spaniard, Domingo Gonzales, who trained large birds for an eventful trip that was to take him eleven days. So popular was this and other stories that moon voyages appeared in over 200 published accounts during the 17th century.

Moon-men were an emerging breed and their strange world was to become the object of increasing interest and speculation. It led to respected astronomers such as Sir William Herschel devoting much of their time to observing the lunar surface.

He himself recorded on two consecutive nights in April, 1787 three bright white spots on the earth-lit side of the moon which he concluded could only have been volcanoes. In 1822 German astronomer Franz von Paula Gruithuisen announced he had discovered a "lunar city" possessing "dark gigantic ramparts". These were to be identified later as consisting of nothing more than haphazard surface ridges.

It was shrewd American news reporter Richard Lock who became the first person to recognize an opportunity for personal fame and fortune, when in 1835 he successfully duped the New York Sun and its readership. In August that year the newspaper was to publish the first of his amazing accounts alleging that Sir John Herschel, son of William, was using a revolutionary new lunar telescope at a site in Southern Africa and through it had observed goat-like creatures ambling about on the moon's surface.

The tale gradually unfolded during the next week as successive editions of the Sun carried ever-more colorful descriptions of flora and fauna, also islands, rivers, birds and beasts. Meanwhile, poor Herschel remained oblivious to these events.

Lock possessed a nifty turn-of-phrase and capitalized on the limitations imposed on communications in the early 19th century. He milked it for all he was worth while the hoax continued, first ensnaring rival newspapers and then even eminent scientists on both sides of the Atlantic.

Readers avidly absorbed every word and were captivated by flowery descriptions of great works supposedly wrought on the lunar surface, such as this:

"A lofty chain of obelisk-shaped or very slender pyramids standing in irregular groups, each composed of about thirty or forty spires, every one of which was perfectly square."

Lock crowned his literary achievement one week later by introducing into the narrative a colorful report of the lunar inhabitants.

These hairy winged creatures were said to be four feet in height and "covered, except on the face, with short and glossy copper-colored hair, lying snugly on their backs. The face, which was of a yellowish flesh-color, was a slight improvement upon that of an orangutan."

A rival newspaper subsequently exposed the whole things as being a hoax, although it took until mid-September before the Sun newspaper, who became willing partners in the deception, grudgingly owned up to it. Herschel for his part was to learn of this duplicity some time later and continued his observations at the Cape apparently somewhat amused at the claims and following furor in both America and Europe.

Lunar observers such as W. H. Pickering spent many years at the turn of this century mapping what he himself often described as "canals" present on the moon's seemingly ever-changing landscape. These mazes of lines were observed to intersect mysterious dark spots, much in the manner of those more famous Martian canals which had been recorded by Schiaparelli and announced to the world in 1877.

Pickering went on to claim that he had identified vegetation, along with "river-beds" and active volcanoes, or geysers. From his vantage point in the hills of Jamaica during 1919-24 the astronomer believed he was witness to the migratory passage of small insects or animals, in their leisurely traversing of the area around the moon's Eratosthenes crater.

Throughout the last 200 years many lunar observers have reported witnessing the brief appearance of inexplicable mists, cloud-like shapes, glows and flashes on a seemingly lifeless gray world. Walter H. Haas, who wrote in 1942 that Sir William Herschel's white spots on the moon might have been the impact flare of a large meteorite, himself observed a "milky luminosity" present on the wall of the crater Tycho.

Astronomer F. H. Thornton reported seeing "a puff of whitish vapor obscuring details for some miles," one February night in 1949.

That same year, Spanish engineer Sixto Campo seriously promoted the theory that a technologically advanced civilization had once waged nuclear war against itself on the lunar surface. Annihilation followed swiftly for all he claimed and the resulting craters remain as testament to the holocaust on a now dead world. However, red glows continue to be observed in the region of the moon's north pole and blue misty glows have been periodically noted near craters at the south pole.

Russian astronomer N. A. Kozyrev has recorded via spectrograms numerous incidents of red transient lunar phenomena, particularly in the 80-mile wide crater known as Alphonsus. It was at this location in 1965 that the final Ranger probe 9 crash-landed.

Aristarchus is not only one of the brightest formations on the moon; it is responsible for more than half the number of reported TLP and has been a proven source for gaseous emissions.

Strange Lunar Shadows
By JJ

The first of the two mysterious incidents I've chosen happened on the night of 3 July 1882. For 45 minutes the residents of Lebanon, Connecticut, were treated to a bizarre lunar display:

"Two pyramidal luminous protuberances appeared on the moon's upper limb. They were not large, but gave the moon a look strikingly like that of a horned owl. These points were a little darker than the rest of the moon's face. They slowly faded away a few moments after their appearance, the one on the right...disappearing first.

About three minutes after their disappearance two black triangular notches were seen on the...lower half of the moon. These points gradually moved toward each other along the moon's edge, and seemed to be...obliterating nearly a quarter of its surface, until they finally met, when the moon's face assumed its normal appearance."

The "pyramidal luminous protuberances" bring to mind the "strange pyramid of light" seen in 1519.

There were also noted similarities in the Sunday Telegraph's report [30 July 2000] that, on 18 June,

"Two large triangular objects were seen flying over Charlesville-Mézières and Villers-Semeuse in eastern France. They made a loud, strange engine noise and swooped down to roof height.

They had metallic bars beneath the engines, with lights at either end. Half an hour earlier and about 200 miles...south-west, Thierry Garnier was... on the outskirts of Gasny when he saw a strong white luminous flash approaching from the east."

Were these two events connected? Were they the triangular UFOs that were written about in the work entitled *Into the Triangle and Beyond*?

I can't believe, though, that the military would've risked flying aircraft so low over urban areas. But would aliens have had such a fit of bravado either? Do the three incidents from different centuries [especially the flashes and fading - think of the Back To The Future films] suggest time travel or a 'time warp'?

It's been said that, what passes for years or even centuries in Earth time, in alien terms may only be a matter of days, weeks or months. This would explain sightings of certain UFO types, such as these triangles, the Flying Wheels, 'cigars', etc, from ancient times onwards. Maybe they're even the same craft and navigators!

The second occurrence took place on 27 January 1912, and was witnessed by Dr. F. B. Harris:

"At 10:30 Eastern time I was surprised to see the left cusp showing the presence of an intensely black body about 250 miles long and 50 wide, allowing 2000 miles from cusp to cusp, in shape like a crow poised.

Of course dark places are here and there on the lunar surface, but not like this. I will say every effort was made to eliminate any error of vision or other mistake... The moon is very tricky. I cannot but think that a very interesting and curious phenomenon has happened."

But what was it?

Well, apparently there exists a high quality photo of a vast starship flying over the Moon, snapped by an astronomer whose name has not been released.

It is said to be an intergalactic craft, several miles long, and capable of carrying thousands at a time! If anyone has any further info, please let me know. An image would be great!!

Some Astounding Lunar Anomaly Images

Below you will find some of the lunar anomalies. These are collected from NASA, Clementine, Hoagland and some other famous sourced. Some of these photos were taken from the Apollo missions from space, others taken from Satellite.

I want you to put things into perspective and think about these images after viewing them.

- They are real

- 2. NASA feared releasing them because most people would be shocked to find that life did exist on the moon

- 3. Keep an open-mind these anomalies do not necessary mean they are alien in nature the Nazis were said to have bases on the moon

Consider this other most of the anomalies are glass since they give off reflections.

Most of the anomalies are HUGE. The bridge is said to be 12 miles, the shard tower is said to be 1.5 miles high and there is said to be cities near mountain ranges the size of LA. These are not camera tricks we are viewing here. There is said to be over 400 unexplained anomalies found on the moon that's enough to show me something is or once existed there.

A photograph of astronaut Alan Bean shows the photographer, Pete Conrad, reflected in Bean's helmet visor. Also reflected in the visor is a "geometric object" hanging several feet above the lunar surface. Also visible is the shadow created by this object.

The object seems to be suspended in a "grid" of surrounding glass-like structure!

The Castle

This strange object, photographed during an Apollo mission, has been named "the castle" by Hoagland.

It seems to have a definite structure, like the remnant wall of some ancient building. The bottom looks as if it has rows of support columns, above which is a high spire. Whatever it is, it's much brighter than the surrounding landscape.

This unusual donut-shaped crater is found in orbit 150 Notice the symmetrical objects that flank the opening on the left side of the crater, and the bull's-eye-like inner crater, which contains two bright objects in the lower part.

April 20, 1972
Lunar Surface
NASA Apollo 16 photo

An elongated, glowing white, cigar shaped craft hovering over a crater - or simply a reflection?

This photo was taken by Apollo-16 just before the April 20, 1972 landing on the Moon. Down left you see the metallic foot of the Lunar Lander. This was taken by Neil Armstrong some say it's a shadow but it does show something very solid and long.

NASA photo AS16-120-19238

The next is possibly the Castle Again but this time in the reflection of the helmet.

The object is casting a shadow and is above the ground so either it's off in the distance or it's something hovering. The castle is said to be a 7 mile large structure. Click below image, a thesis of the artifact and better photo.

CHAPTER TEN

UNDERGROUND ALIEN BASES AROUND THE WORLD

There are many stories about supposed underground alien basis across the world. The following list covers just a few of those that are either known or at least strongly rumored[53].

AFGHANISTAN
"There is an ancient legend among the Hindus of India that tells of a civilization of immense beauty beneath central Asia. Several underground cities are said to be located north of the Himalayan Mountains, possibly in Afghanistan, or under the Hindu Kush. This subterranean Shangri-La is inhabited by a race of golden people who seldom communicate with the surface world. From time to time, they travel into our land through tunnels that stretch in many directions. Entrances to the tunnels are believed to be hidden in several of the ancient cities of the Orient.

---

[53] For this list I am greatly indebted to The Hollow Earth Insider and writer Rick Osman.
http://www.bibliotecapleyades.net/offlimits/esp_offlimits_7.htm

Tunnel entrances are said to be in Eldora and the Ajanta caverns in the Chand ore Mountain range of India."

ANTARCTICA
Admiralty Mountains – Mt. Levis

The primary function of this base is as a weather regulator. Human experiments are also conducted to make bodies tough. There is also radio interference and checking communications of Southern Hemisphere. There are also numerous levels to this facility one of which contains a highly sophisticated Atomic Reactor. Unconventional Atomic weapons for attack on other planets are researched and manufactured at this facility.

Sor Rondane Mountains.

This is another multi-level underground military facility.

ARGENTINA
Corcovado

This is a planetary watch post.

Area Villa de Maria

This facility is dedicated to investigating the results of their experiments in the Andes. The size of the facility is unknown but there is said to be a sizable human research staff. There are also indications that a large number of kidnapped prisoners are also held here.

Area Cerro Las Tortolas

There are said to be two bases in this area. There is a political base with responsibility over Argentina, Uruguay, Paraguay and Brazil. The base here is said to be staffed primarily by aliens.

AUSTRALIA
Pine Gap

There is a multi-level underground installation that is said to be used for special aircraft testing. There is also said to be a UFO base. There is a high level security in force here. It is also said to be a shipping point for the shipping of particle beam weapons to the Moon Base.

BRAZIL

One tunnel in Brazil is near Ponte Grosse in the state of Parana. (Fruit orchards were seen here.) Another entrance in Brazil is near Rincon, state of Parana. Also, in the state of Santa Catarina, Brazil, near the city of Joinville there is a mountain containing an entrance to the tunnels. (Santa Catarina is an area alive with subterranean activity, including strange 'singing' from underground.) Another entrance in Brazil is in the state of Sao Paulo near Concepiao. Still another entrance in Santa Catarina near Gaspar has subterranean fruit orchards.

"The states of Santa Catarina and Parana, Brazil are honeycombed by a network of Atlantean tunnels that lead to subterranean cities."

CANADA
Calgary

There is said to be an underground facility located here that researches bovine genetics.

The Nahanni Valley (Canada) Entrance

This covers 250 square miles in the southern end of the Mackenzie Mountains of Canada. It lies almost 550 miles due west of Fort Simpson on the Mackenzie River of northwest Canada. Hot springs and sulfur geysers keep the valley warmer than the surrounding areas by about 30 degrees year -round (the valley is above 60 degrees latitude), making it perpetually mist-covered. This valley is inhabited only by animals as people entering the valley are usually found headless and quite dead. The Indian tribes of the area avoid this valley. (These tribes include the Ojibways, the Slave, the Dogribs, the Stoney, the Beavers and the Chipweyans.) This valley is often referred to as "the Valley of the Headless Men.

Canadian UFO Bases

Entrances at Lake Ontario possible underwater UFO bases/cities. Toronto Tunnels leading to subterranean city. Newfoundland Condemned Iron Mine connects with tunnels. Lake Ontario "Lights" Orange-colored spheres have been seen coming out of/diving into Lake Ontario. The area of highest activity is between Oakville and Toronto. There may be a connection to the Lakeview Hydro-electric plant, as many of these UFOs have been seen heading in that direction.

Toronto Entrance

There is a small opening to the underground tunnels off Parliament Street in downtown Toronto. (The entrance is between two apartment buildings, and leads to the tunnels via the sewers.) The underground city (abandoned?) beneath Toronto has its center beneath Gerrard Street and Church Street. Above this area, strange magnetic effects have been observed.

This corner of Gerrard & Church streets has a higher accident rate than anywhere else in Toronto. It is believed that underground equipment utilizing powerful magnetic fields -which have caused many strange magnetic effects in houses near this intersection- are responsible for the bizarre equipment failures that often are the cause of these accidents.

The Indians near Toronto have legends of these tunnels.

Newfoundland Iron Mine Entrance

After one of the Iron Mines in Newfoundland Province had been dug deeper than any other, strange happenings caused the mine to be shut down. The mining town in which this mine is located is near the Newfoundland-Quebec Border. This mine, having been condemned, is off-limits, and the police DO enforce this. Sneaking in late at night seems to be the only way to gain entrance.

Mount Greenough

Located at this location is another base about which little is known.

CAROLINA ISLANDS AND MALAYSIA

Paul Doerr, in issue number 6 of his Newsletter Unknown, related the tradition concerning a race of human giants which, according to stories in the Carolinas islands and especially Papua, allegedly went underground in ancient times. Once inhabitants of a lost island-continent called "Chamat," they will, according to legend, one day emerge. This legend is wide-spread throughout Malaysia, which incidentally contains the largest "officially recognized" cavern chamber, the "Sarowak Chamber" on the island of Borneo in the Malaysian islands.

It is said to be 230 ft. wide by 980 ft. long and nowhere less than 270 ft. high, large enough to easily hold within itself the two previous contenders for the world's largest official chamber - Carlsbad's "Big Room" in New Mexico and the "Salle de la Verna" in the Pierre Saint- Martin caverns in France. Yankee stadium could fit in one end of the Sarowak chamber with room to spare!

The Book of Dyzan, which has been translated from ancient manuscripts, tells of intellectually sophisticated humans from an ancient earth-born society who abandoned the surface of the earth, "depriving the impure human race of their knowledge," and leaving in flying craft to rejoin their land "of iron and metal."

CHINA

If we turn to Chinese folklore, we find a time lapse of hundreds of years. There is a book entitled "*The Report Concerning the Cave Heavens and Lands of Happiness in Famous Mountains*," by Tu Kuang-t'ing, who lived from 850 to 933 A.D.

This book lists ten 'cave heavens' and thirty-six 'small cave heavens' that were supposed to exist beneath the mountains in China. Here are the reported experiences of a man who entered a passageway leading to one of these cave heavens:

After walking ten miles, he suddenly found himself in a beautiful land 'with a clear blue sky, shining pinkish clouds, fragrant flowers, densely growing willows, towers the color of cinnabar, pavilions of red jade, and far flung palaces.' He was met by a group of lovely, seductive women, who brought him to a house of jasper, and played him beautiful music while he drank 'a ruby-red drink and a jade-colored juice.' Just as he felt the urge to let himself be seduced, he remembered his family and returned to the passageway.

Led by a strange light that danced before him, he walked back through the cave to the outer world; but when he reached his home village, he did not recognize anyone he saw, and when he arrived at his house, he met his own descendants of nine generations hence. They told him that one of their ancestors had disappeared into a cavern three hundred years before and had never been seen again.'

ENGLAND
Bentwaters

Meriwith Hill

Rudloe Manor Wiltshire, just outside of Bath, Southern England

The Staffordshire, England Entrance

Somewhere in Staffordshire, England a lonely field exists in which a laborer discovered a large iron plate beneath the dirt. The "hatch" was large and oval, with an iron ring mounted on it. This entrance led into the tunnels. The field is in a valley surrounded on almost all sides by woods. The laborer was digging a trench for some purpose. The incident was reported in "A History of Staffordshire" by Dr. Plot, who wrote the book in the late 1700s. It may be possible to find the entrance if it can be ascertained exactly which valley the laborer was digging in.

Suffolk

EGYPT

Dr. Earlyne Chaney, in an article titled 'Odyssey Into Egypt,' in her occult-oriented magazine Voice of Astara (May, 1982) tells of a discovery she and researcher Bill Cox was shown in Egypt. These were two tunnels, neither of which had been fully explored. One was in the temple of Edfu between Luxor and Cairo in the ruins of El Tuna Gabel; and the other near Zozer's Step Pyramid at Cairo near Memphis-Saqqarah, within the tomb of the Bull, called "Serapium".

The Egyptian government sealed both tunnels because of fears of certain archaeologists who alleged that they "lead too deeply down into the depths of the earth," and because they found the earth to be "honeycombed with passages leading off into other depths," and the possibility of explorers becoming lost.

If such labyrinths do exist, then it may explain one story which alleged that men dressed like "ancient Egyptians" have been seen deep in unexplored tunnels near Cairo, as well as possible confirmation of the story which appeared in Nevada Aerial Research's Leading Edge publication to the effect that the U.S.(?) Government secretly maintains a huge base within a cavern of tremendous size (several miles in diameter) beneath the desert sands of Egypt.

Could this tie in with the vague references to a subterranean society(s) referred to by certain people 'in the know' which is/are known as the 'Phoenix Empire' and/or the 'Gizeh People'?

GREENLAND
Area Cape Farvel

There is an underground base located here that is said to be staffed by at least 20 extra-terrestrials and 50 aborigines.

ICELAND
Jokulsaarglifur National Park

There is an underground facility located here from which tunnels run to numerous locations.

IRAN

There is said to be a very large underground military installation with multiple levels. From this facility tunnels run to several different destinations.

IRAQ

There is a multi-level military facility located somewhere in Iraq.

MEXICO
The Liyobaa Cave Entrance

This was sealed off by Catholic Priests who believed it to be an entrance to "Hell."

"The village of 'Liyobaa' or to translate, 'The Cavern of Death,' was located in the province of Zapoteca, somewhere near the ancient village of 'Mictlan' or the village of the 'Underworld.

"The Cavern of Death was actually located in the last chamber of an eight chamber building or temple. This temple had four rooms above the ground and four more important chambers built below the surface of the Earth. This building was located in "Theozapotlan," and the tunnel entrance led one beneath a mountain."

MALTA
The Maltese Cave Entrance

This entrance is located on the island of Malta, near the small village of "Casal Paula." (This village is built on the "Corradino" plateau, and overlooks the capitol town of Malta, "Valletta," as well as Grand Harbour.) In 1902, workmen digging a well in Casal Paula fell into a subterranean cavern. The well was being dug for a house on "Hal Saflienti," the main street in Casal Paula. The cavern the workers had fallen into connected with an entire complex of caves and tunnels. This entrance is known as the "Hypogeum of Hal Saflienti." (In Latin, "Hypogeum" is the name for an underground structure.)

The tunnels under the Hypogeum have been sealed off even since a school took 30 students into the caves and disappeared, guide and all. Search parties were never able to locate any trace of the people and children.

NORTH POLE

There is said to be an underground base located here that serves as a regulator of communications between the other bases.

NORWAY
Finmark

This is a base dedicated to atomic energy research.

RUSSIA
Ramenki

There is a multi-level underground base located here. This facility is said to be over 500 acres in size and could hold 120,000 people. From this location there are said be tunnels leading to Moscow.

Yamantan Mountain, Russia Belorelsk, Southern Urals

There is a huge complex concealed here that is said to be the same size as the Washington area inside the beltway. From this location are said to be tunnels running to unknown places.

Tundra-Peninsula of Kola

The underground base located here specializes in implants in the body and the mind. It is believed that this facility is staffed by over fifty extra-terrestrials, over fifty humans as well as over 100 hybrids who serve as helpers to the research scientists. At any given time there are 100 patients and over 500 animals.

Siberia – area Chatanga where the rivers Kotuja and the Cheta meet.

There is a multi-level underground base located at this location which is said to be staffed by over 60 extra-terrestrials, almost 50 humans and 80 hybrids who serve as aids to the scientists.

Egveknot

The location of another underground base containing a joint alien/human staff.

SOUTH AMERICA

Karl Brugger, in his book *The Chronicle of Akakor*[54], gives the history - as given to the author by one of their chiefs - of the Ugha Mongulala tribesman, whose ancestors were allegedly part of a vast empire which covered South America in ancient times.

Some of these ancient people, the chief claimed, left the planet in aerial vessels to explore other parts of the solar system and beyond, leaving behind vast subterranean cities beneath the Andes Mountains and western Brazil.

---

[54] Brugger, Karl, The Chronicle of Akakor, Delecorte Press, N. Y.

In 1971, due to the constant encroachment of white settlers or invaders into their territory, 30,000 survivors of the Ugha Mongulala allegedly escaped to this ancient system of underground cities, consisting of 13 separate subterranean complexes all connected by tunnels, one of which is said to extend to Lima, and others of which are located throughout the Andes Mountain range of Peru.

Saga Magazine's UFO Annual [980, p4], under the heading 'Cave Martians', described a bizarre encounter with subterranean creatures which seemed to have consisted of some type of automaton-like forms, perhaps on a reconnaissance mission from an underground civilization. The story involved a tunnel near Xucurus, Argentina(?), some 90 miles from Buenos Aires.

The tunnel was discovered by agriculturalist Gerardo Cordeire, and found to contain nine connecting passages and strange inscriptions on the walls.

From it's entrance "men nine feet tall, green, with antennas on their heads, and square legs" were seen to emerge, and which, according to hundreds of witnesses from the town and nearby locals, resembled enormous "portable radios."

SWEDEN
Norbottens Lan

The underground base located at this site is dedicated to poltical control.

TURKEY

Thirty six underground cities have been discovered so far in Cappadocia with some going down eight levels.

Some of these cities can hold a population of thousands. The ventilation systems are so efficient that even eight floors down the air is still fresh. Thirty vast underground cities and tunnel complexes have also been found near Derinkuya in Turkey.

ZIMBABWE
<u>Mt. Inyangani</u>

This is a rather large underground facility that is said to actually serve as a maintenance and tech center. This base looks like an overhaul and maintenance unit. There is a lot of equipment, parts are welded in a vacuum area with window area then parts are used. A grayish white powder is pasted on both parts then fused.

CHAPTER ELEVEN

UNDERGROUND BASES IN THE UNITED STATES

These areas were found off a government map showing just some of the underground bases in the United States[55]. Clearly, much more than we ever dreamed of can be found beneath our feet.

• **EDWARDS AIR FORCE BASE**- :From Edwards Air Force Base a tunnel goes to Vandenberg Air Force Base From Vandenberg you back up to Edwards and go Southeast to subterranean base at a place that the map designates as Cat., which probably means Catalina Island, showing a flying saucer there so alien space crafts are probably seen there.

---

[55] For this list I am greatly indebted to The Hollow Earth Insider and writer Rick Osman.
http://www.bibliotecapleyades.net/offlimits/esp_offlimits_7.htm

There is a map shows an underground base and a tunnel going into it at a place called 29 Palms.

- The next place on the map where an underground base is, is the Chocolate Mts.

- There appears to be a site in Nevada at Tonopah, Area 51 at Groom Lake, and a place designated as COG AFB.

- In Arizona we have sites at Wickiup and Page.

- Utah there is one at Salt Lake City (R&D AFB).

- There is one in Riverton "M", Denver, Colorado, Colorado Springs, COG Creedo and Delta.

- In New Mexico they are at Dulce, Taos, Los Alanos, ALB, AFB, Datil and Carlsbad.

- In Texas there is one at Lubbock. Denton "908" (C.O.G) seems to have an isolated one, Ft. Stockton and in Old Mexico there is one at Chihuahua.

- Tulsa Oklahoma has one and just NE of there we appear to have one with a saucer coming out of it.

- Hutchison AFB Kansas has one.

ARIZONA

GRAND CANYON –
      There are a lot of stories about cave[s] near the confluence of the Colorado and Little Colorado Rivers. Hopi legends say that their ancestors once lived underground with a friendly race of "ant people" [not to be confused with the sinister "mantis" people described by several abductees], but some of their kind turned to sorcery and made an alliance with lizard or serpent men known as the "two hearts", which dwelt in still deeper caverns below. The "flood" of evil and violence forced the peaceful Hopi's to the surface world. An explorer named G. E. Kincaid claimed to have found "one of" the ancient caves, in which were reportedly discovered Oriental, Egyptian & Central American type artifacts.
      Smithsonian archaeologists S. A. Jordan and associates also explored the man-made cavern with hundreds of rooms, enough to hold over 50,000 people. The underground city is about 42 miles up river from El Tovar Crystal Canyon and Crystal Creek, and about 2000 feet above the river bed on the east wall.
      John Rhodes after 3 years of field research reportedly discovered the Grand Canyon city, which is now being used as a museum for elitist groups and has lower levels that are being used by "super secret black book operatives", which can only be entered via a stainless steel door at the bottom of a stairwell deep within the "city" that is "guarded by a very lonely soldier staring into the

darkness... dressed in a white jumpsuit and armed only with an M16 assault rifle to ward off his imagination[56]."

SEDONA –

Famous for its massive vortexes, Sedona is claimed to be an ancient colony of the Lemurians. According to Commander X, there are reports of a joint-operational underground city and facility under the Enchantment Resort in Boyton Canyon, where clone-like men in black have been seen, along with unusual electromagnetic vortex phenomena[57].

SUPERSTITION MTS. –

Several people claim to have had experiences with all types of alien beings inhabiting underground levels below the Superstitution Mts. east of Phoenix. Early reports speak of humans and human-dwarfs inhabiting the caverns of the region, although in the 20th century reports of reptilian and grey type aliens have increased. Some encounters involve white-greys from Epsilon Bootes, humanoid or reptiloid "deros" in black hooded cloaks using abducted/programmed humans above and below as mind slaves or worse; reptilian humanoids with integrated human

---

[56] : ARIZONA GAZETTE, March 12, 1909 & April 5, 1909; Robert Morning Sky; John Rhodes

[57] David Icke, Children of the Matrix notes that Sedona is associated to UFO activities with a reptilian underground base where members of the reptilian race work with their human or part-human puppets in the Illuminati on the scientific and genetic agenda. The base would appear to be under Boynton Canyon in Sedona. This is not far from the reservation of the Hopi tribe, which has Lemurian connections

DNA abducting and raping women; and various other regressive underground scenarios[58].

FORT HUACHUCA, ARIZONA – Fort Huachuca had and possibly still does have a large underground base and tunnel system that is occupied by a Top Secret communications and cryptography unit. NSA either commands or has peripheral use of the facility. The Arizona military site is also one of the many designated detainment (concentration) camps authorized by our government, under the Homeland Security Act, if martial law is necessarily declared.

ARKANSAS

CUSHMAN –

Caverns west and west-north-west of the town are legendary for stories of deep cavern systems, encounters with hairy humanoids with an attitude, giant serpents and insects, deadly gas pockets, strange electro-magnetic phenomena and unexplained disappearances. One of these is "Blowing Cave" which lies in the mining area NW of Cushman and is located 1/4 mile north of a road leading west from Cushman, one of several caverns in the area, some of them possibly connecting at the deeper levels.\

Between the large entrance and an underground lake far back in the cave is a trail that winds through an area of rubble or "breakdown". The trail is intersected by a crack in the earth [between the entrance and the lake] that,

---

[58] Kaye Kiziar; Commander X; Brian Scott; Steve Brodie; Hank Krastman

if followed into the breakdown, widens enough to enter. This chasm is reportedly an entrance to the endless networks of the alien underworld[59].

CALIFORNIA

<u>Indian Legends of California</u>

The Modoc tribe tell that ' thousands of snows ago, there was a great storm over Mt. Shasta. The Great Spirit, who lived within the mountain, sent his youngest daughter out to speak to the storm and tell it to stop blowing so hard, or else the mountain might blow over. He also told her not to stick her head out the top of the mountain, or the wind could catch her long, red hair, and blow her away. The girl, however, having never seen the sea, was overcome with curiosity and stuck her head out of the top of the mountain to see it.

As her father the Great Spirit had warned, her long, red hair caught the mighty wind, and she was blown away. Fortunately a group of Grizzly bears found her and took her in. These Grizzly bears were not like modern Grizzlies, however, they were more like humans, walking on two feet, and when the Great Spirit's daughter came of age, she married the oldest Grizzly's son. Their children were then a combination of spirit and animal, having the nature of both; they were the first Modocs.'

There have been tales of strange-looking, robed persons emerging from the forests and coming into nearby

---

[59] Charles Marcoux - -
George Wight - D. A. Lopez; TRIP TO A CUSHMAN CAVERN

towns surround Mt. Shasta to trade gold nuggets for supplies:

These odd looking persons were not only peculiar in their dress and different in attire from any costume ever seen on the American Indian, and especially in the California Indian, but distinctive in features and complexion; tall, graceful and agile, having the appearance of being quite old and yet exceedingly virile.'

A protrusion in the center of their very high foreheads was said to be a special organ enabling them to communicate by telepathy. When approached by townspeople, the Lemurians would apparently vanish into thin air.

According to the Brotherhood of the White Temple in Sedalia, Colorado in a book entitled "Mysteries of Mount Shasta", it is Atlanteans, not Lemurians, who inhabit Mt. Shasta. Though the Lemurians had indeed created vast, underground pleasure palaces beneath the mountain, they had lost their freedom in a great war with the Atlanteans, and remain imprisoned by the Atlanteans in their pleasure palaces even today.

"After their retreat, the Atlantean victors sealed the entrance and established an elaborate guard system which prohibits the Lemurians to ever escape their bondage. The Atlanteans, Dr. Doreal states, still reside in their colony beneath Mt. Shasta and commute every three months by strange cigar-shaped airships to an area in the South Pacific in order to check the sealed entrance of the imprisoned Lemurians."

It is these aircraft, some say, that accounts for the occasional appearances of UFOs above Mt. Shasta.

The Paihute Indians of the southwest USA claim that a Greek or Egyptian-like race first colonized the massive caverns within the Panamint Mts. thousands of years ago [one source claims the base was established around 2500 B.C., which is incidentally about 600 years following the beginnings of the rise of Egyptian intellectual culture] when Death Valley was part of an inland sea connected to the Pacific Ocean.

When the sea dried up these people -- who were described as wearing flowing robes draped over one shoulder, head-bands holding back their long dark hair, and bronze-golden skin -- out of necessity began to develop their collective knowledge and intellect and soon afterwards began to construct "silvery flying canoes". At first these flying machines possessed wings, were relatively small, and flew with a dipping movement and a loud 'whirring' noise. As time passed the ships became wingless, grew larger in size, and flew ever more smoothly and silently.

Eventually these people, the HAV-MUSUVS moved their civilization into still deeper caverns which they had discovered farther underground, and commenced to explore the nearby planets and eventually other star systems as their own technological explosion began to refine every aspect of their society. These Hav-musuvs have apparently had interplanetary or interstellar travel for 3000-4000 years since they first developed their flying machines. Could they have been one of the many native-terranian "ancient astronaut" civilizations which apparently had colonized Lyra and other systems?

The story of the Panamints was related by a Navaho Indian by the name of Oga-Make, who in turn heard it from an old Paihute medicine man.

29 PALMS MARINE BASE –

Beneath 29 Palms Marine Base are said to be Underground facilities involved with recovered alien technology and research. Also a geological anomaly in the area created by sea water rushing in to underlying caverns when the area was under water, creating a tunnel-like structure from which UFO's have been seen to emerge. Attempts of Army personnel to send cameras down resulted in the camera cables being "cut", and attempts to send military speleonauts down on ropes resulted in the explorers being exposed to a noxious blue gas which had apparently been released from below to prevent them from descending[60].

ANAHEIM –

On Nov. 3, 1989, radio talk show host Ken Hudnall announced his intention to take a group to visit an ancient underground city 60 miles from Anaheim[61].

BAKERSFIELD –

In 1972 Wanda Lockwood of Bakersfield, CA reported that in 1970 she was playing with her son in his bedroom when what sounded like a large steel hammer struck the concrete basement floor 3 times. Her child Danny was so surprised that he began to cry. Having heard

---

[60] Val Valerian; 29 PALMS MARINE BASE
[61] THE LEADING EDGE; KEN HUDNaLL

a similar noise several months earlier beneath her living room, Wanda was curious and put her ear to the bedroom floor and clearly heard "the roar of machinery".

She took a hammer and began to pound the bedroom [basement?] floor in a 1-2-3, 1-2-3 manner until 5 minutes later a "being" beneath the floor began to tap back in the same 1-2-3, 1-2-3 manner. She could hear a series of noises and knocks and then she faintly heard MEN talking to each other, but the voices were too muffled to understand.

In later months she would again hear the machinery when placing her ear to the floor, but never again the men's voices[62].

BARSTOW –

Camp Irwin is located near Barstow, CA. . Reports of several tunnels below the Camp Irwin area, one of which is an abandoned mine at the bottom of which is an "earth crack" which leads to a tunnel that connects with a massive underground river about a quarter of a mile wide, one of at least five subterranean rivers which rise and fall with the tides, suggesting the source of origin being a large underground sea below the dry basins of Utah and Nevada. One of these reportedly runs below Kokoweef and Dorr peaks near the SW flank of the Ivanpah Mts. NW of Needles, California. These underground rivers are said to

---

[62] FATE Magazine, April, 1972

empty into the Pacific or Gulf of California via large aqua caves near the base of the continental slopes[63].

Leon Davidson, in an early issue of Flying Saucers Magazine, spoke of a large network of "underground tunnels in the California desert, at Camp Irwin, near Barstow." This may tie-in with an item related by a Los Angeles municipal water director, as related in an early issue of Richard Toronto's Shavertron letter-zine, stating that this water director knew of 5 large underground rivers which ran beneath the Mojave desert, and that die-traces showed that at least one of these emptied into the Pacific ocean through openings in the continental slopes (One source stated that such a river exited in the Gulf of California).

Other sources speak of a "Kokoweef" river-system which is alleged to lie below Kokoweef peak just east of Fort Irwin, which looked- -according to it's alleged discoverer, a Mr. Earl Dorr, and a few "Indians" who also claimed to have been in it--like a "Grand Canyon" underground. It allegedly consists of a river chasm generally 500 ft. wide and over a thousand feet high-deep, sided by steep tiered-shelved underground cliffs, huge stalactites and cataracts. Also, the alluvial sands on the 'beaches' along the river, which allegedly hold a large percentage of gold dust, are said to be several feet deep.

The entrance to this cavern was allegedly dynamited shut by Mr. Dorr to protect anyone else from getting to "his" gold. There is in fact evidence that Dorr did

---

[63] DEPTHS OF THE EARTH, by William R. Halliday; Leon Davidson; Richard Toronto; FORT IRWIN; CALIFORNIA'S UNDERGROUND RIVER CANYONS

dynamite shut the lower level of 'Kin Sabe' cave in Kokoweef Peak, and there are present-day attempts to break through into this underground system. The water of the river allegedly rose and fell with the tides, suggesting that a very large body of water might exist upstream, that is if Dorr's account as well as the accounts of the Indians were not fabricated).

The municipal water director, according to the Shavertron article, spoke with a man who claimed that he was hired several years ago by the government to look for water sources for Ft. Irwin. He alleged to have explored an old mine in the area and found that deep down, the shaft intersected with an ancient earth fault or chasm- like cave which continued horizontally for a considerable distance. This government employee followed the chasm and allegedly emerged onto the bank of a huge underground river-cave over a quarter of a mile wide!

The tremendous water flow - possibly originating from the waters that apparently disappear beneath the Great Basin, the Nevada and Mojave deserts -could have 'fed' the water needs of all of Southern California.

DEEP SPRINGS –

Deeps Springs, due east of San Jose and next to the California-Nevada border, is named after a small spring fed lake, within which government divers have reportedly discovered an underground river which they have followed for approximately 27 miles in the direction of Las Vegas, although it is uncertain whether or how much of this is walkable.

Evidence of Alien Contact

Deep Springs, according to an agent who was part of a secret CIA paramilitary force called "Yellow Fruit" or "YF" based at the Nevada Test Site [where they are working with "blond" humanoid aliens in an effort to fight the Greys at deep springs], is the basing area of a large nest of grey aliens and communist-homosexual human collaborators who are using the "National Resources Defense Council" as a front for their agency, and who are involved in an electromagnetic war with the "benevolent ones" who have made allies within the Nevada Test Site, who serve as advisors to intelligence agencies that are turning against the greys as a result of betrayals of joint-operation treaties.

However there are still intelligence agencies under alien control working at the Nevada Test Site and especially within the deeper underground levels [the benevolent ones and their allies essentially having gained the "upper ground"], however the whole scenario is a mess and "out of control", largely because of the military-industrial "machine" itself which has become so compartmentalized and secretive [even to the exclusion of Congressional oversight] that the true patriots don't have the freedom or backup to do much damage against their underground nemesis, mainly because of the limitations imposed upon them by fraternal oaths, mental programming, and military security clearances.

It is basically every man for himself, UNTIL at least the PUBLIC and CONGRESS gets involved and adds their support to the patriots who are literally dying on the front lines in this battle with an alien nemesis which has infiltrated the very core of the military-industrial complex.

Men In Black, by the way, have also been seen at Deep Springs. Also several "stand-offs" allegedly exist throughout the world, the Deep Springs - Nevada Test Site stand-off being possibly the largest and most critical. Gravity anomaly maps also suggest the existence of massive caverns beneath the area.

Agent "YF" cited the following coordinates as locations of Deep Springs extension facilities, in most cases near the bases of mountains near which portals to the underground installations exist: N 37 22 30 - E 117 58 0; N 38 21 0 - E 115 35 0; N 35 39 0 - E 114 51 0; and also Yucca Lake: N 37 0 30 - E 116 7 0[64].

CADIZ –

The late Earl Gambrel tells how he was transported by an alien craft one night from the outskirts of Barstow to an area just 2 miles NW of Bonanza Springs, some 13 miles from Cadiz and just south of the Clipper mountain area. He found [or was shown] a cave or tunnel in the side of a hill near a natural rock arch and a peak which looks like it has "a black railroad car on top of it." After considerable travel underground at a 30 degree descent, he reached an underground city with streets and houses filled with large crystals, now abandoned. He also heard of another man who reportedly found the cave and told others about it, but who was killed shortly thereafter[65].

---

[64] John Lear; LEADING EDGE Newsletter, Dec. 1989 - Jan. 1990
[65] : John Winston; Map Location of Cadiz

CHINA LAKE –

A woman name "Diane" claimed that she has had numerous alien encounters since childhood. During one encounter she was taken to a joint alien-military facility deep beneath the China Lake Naval Weapons Test Center via a magnetic elevator to a huge facility where she observed numerous humans and animals in cages that had been bio-genetically altered. Also, there are possibly a massive underground facilities beneath Argus and/or Southeast Peaks NW of Trona in the China Lake Reserve.[66]

CLEAR LAKE –

According to Robert K. Newkirk, northern California's "Clear Lake has many underground caverns [leading under Mt. Konocti] that we know have no endings and others that run to San Francisco Bay[67]."

EDWARDS AIR FORCE BASE –

The "Haystack" bluff or butte near the launch area reportedly holds underground levels and surface pylons where pulse beam and stealth research is being carried out. Haystack Butte is reportedly the central hub of massive underground activity, with underground connections to other facilities. Witnesses who have described alien activity there have died under mysterious circumstances. Also reports of a 50 mile underground tube-shuttle linking Edwards AFB with the Tahachapi facility, and an ongoing excavation below the base down past 9000 feet, with

---

[66] ALIEN MAGIC, by William F. Hamilton III; UNDERGROUND BASES AND TUNNELS, by Richard Sauder;
[67] AMAZING STORIES; Mt. Konocti

underground facilities being monitored by hovering remote-controlled basketball sized metallic spheres capable of electromagnetically monitoring the encephalographic waves of base workers and visitors and thus anticipate their intents[68].

EL PASO MOUNTAINS –

Below Iron Canyon and Gofer, NW of Garlock [over a dozen miles north of Mojave, California near the El Paso Mountains], there have been reports of alien beings who control deadly "machines" which stalk the surface, especially near Iron Canyon, at night. Also reports of secret government monitoring activity and also there is a major electromagnetic 'vortex' energy field in the area[69].

ESSEX –

Jack Mitchell, founder of Mitchell Caverns [18 miles north of Essex, which is 28 miles west of Needles and 111 miles east of Barstow on Route 66] claimed that while exploring a shaft called "The Cave of the Winding Stair" in or near Mitchell Caverns, he was lowered down to a ledge 500 feet below, from where he set fire to a gasoline soaked sock with a rock in it, and watched it disappear into the shaft without seeing it hit anything[70].

HELENDALE –

---

[68] B.S.R.F. Newsletter, Dec. 1990; The LEADING EDGE Newsletter, May 1989; William F. Hamilton, III
[69] UFO ANNUAL magazine [year uncertain]; El Paso Mts.; Garlock Fault Zone
[70] CAVEMAN, the autobiography of Jack Mitchell; Mitchell's Caverns

SW of Barstow there is a Lockheed facility known as the RCS [Radar Cross Section] test range, and also known as the "Helendale" facility. A massive underground base site and C.O.G. [Continuity Of Government] facility, located 6 miles north of Helendale auxiliary airport. There are several underground openings, especially in the northern end. Also there is a 100 foot pylon for testing antigravity prototypes. Some of these pylons are retractable and rise from or sink into openings in the ground[71].

BETWEEN HOPLAND & LAKEPORT –

Edward John spoke of an area midway between the two cities [in the area of the Krishna temple] and somewhat south, where the following has been reported: space-time distortions, attempted attacks by alien creatures at night, an atmosphere of terror covering a 30 mile area, black automobiles disappearing into cliffs, strange voices in an unknown language coming out of thin air, cars mysteriously stalling and starting, rumors of a "bottomless cave" with a stone staircase leading downward, unexplained disappearances of "government vehicles" along the Hopland - Lakeport road, and mysterious deaths among residents of a nearby valley. Also a 1990 magnetic survey identified a large gap in the magnetic field near Lakeport and Mt. Konocti, suggesting a large cavernous expanse below[72].

JUNE LAKE –

---

[71] HUFON REPORT, Nov. 1992; Helendale Facility
[72] AMAZING STORIES magazine, May 1946 - Dec. 1946; Route from Hopland[*star] to Lakeport

Jack Peterson reported an encounter near June Lake where he reportedly observed a small humanoid being exiting from a cone-shaped machine which had emerged from the depths of the earth, and which disappeared into the earth after the "alien" had re-entered the craft[73].

LANCASTER –

There is a collaboration between Northrup, McDonnel-Douglas and Lockheed that is developing and testing antigravity air and/or space craft in massive underground facilities. Abductees report being taken to these elaborate multi-billion dollar underground complexes where they have seen human military personnel working with grey aliens and in some cases reptilian humanoids. Glowing discs, triangles, boomerangs, elongated shapes, spheres and other types of antigravity craft have been seen flying or hovering in the area, as well as black unmarked helicopters[74].

LANDERS.

About a dozen miles north of Yucca Valley is Giant Rock, thought to be the largest free-standing boulder in the world. It covers 5800 sq. ft. and is 7 stories high. It was used in ancient times for seances by Native American chiefs. Frank Critzer was the first modern individual to excavate rooms from beneath Giant Rock. According to Hank Krastman, Frank stated that in the process of his

---

[73] SHAVERTRON, issue No.14; June Lake, California
[74] HUFON REPORT, Nov. 1992; Michael Lindemann & Michael Riconosciuto

excavations he "had stumbled onto some unusual glass-lined tunnels under ground which went down real deep".

Critzer hollowed out 400 square feet of rooms from under the north side. Deputies from Riverside county [Giant Rock is in San Bernardino county] during WWII tried to apprehend Frank for questioning as a possible German spy [there were several in the area at the time] but when Frank barricaded himself in his "home" the deputies threw in a tear gas grenade, which ignited a pile of dynamite under his table that was used for excavation. The deep "glass" tunnels may have been buried in that explosion. Frank was killed, and newspapers held with the spy story even though the FBI told George Van Tassel it was not true.

George restored some of the rooms under the rock, where he claimed to have had meetings with human ET's who claimed to be members of a Solar system Tribunal on one of the moons of Saturn. Van Tassel was instructed to build the domed "Integratron" near the Giant Rock, with the belief that the weight of the rock pressing down on the sand-quartz below created an electromagnetic field similar to the one created about 7 feet above the apex of the Great pyramid, generated by the massive weight pressing down on the quartz-laden stones. After George passed away the "government" blew up the underground chamber[75].

MT. LASSEN –

Two young men reported the discovery of a glazed tunnel behind an outcropping of rock at about the 7500 ft.

---

[75] INTERNATIONAL UFO Magazine, article by Hank Krastman; Giant Rock & the Integratron

level on the slopes of Mt. Lassen. They explored the cavern using a strange tunnel vehicle and were captured by men dressed as surface people who were known as the "horlocks", humans under the total mind-control of some alien force, only to be rescued by an underground resistance force. Others have reported abductions near Lassen by a human - reptilian collaboration[76].

LLANO –

A large McDonnel-Douglass facility based at the old Grey Butte Airport, about 6 miles SW of El Mirage dry lake and 9 miles NE of Llano. Also contains pylons upon which various aerodynamic hulls are placed for stealth and other design tests. Often the objects atop the pylons have been seen to glow at various intensities[77].

LOS ANGELES –

On Feb. 12, 1953, witnesses observed an automobile enter the throat of a storm drain near Willowbrook and Greenleaf Avenues in Los Angeles. Police followed the fresh tire-tred marks into the tunnel for 7 miles, while other police & flood control workers continued the search by dropping through manhole covers. The search continued until midnight, until 7 miles up the drain the tracks VANISHED. "In the muddy silt covering the floor of the drain, the tire-tred marks were sharp and fresh... then no more tracks[78]."

---

[76] AMAZING STORIES magazine, Dec. 1946; Mt. Lassen Natl. Park
[77] HUFON REPORT, Nov. 1992; Map of Llano, California; the Yano [sic/i.e. Llano] Facility & Aliens
[78] STRANGE DISAPPEARANCES, by Brad Steiger

LOS ANGELES –

A legendary underground city, now flooded, is said to lie below the Los Angeles Public Library and surrounding areas. Patterned after the shape of a lizard, the city is said to be connected to Mt. Shasta, and was built by an ancient race that revered reptiles. Although filled with gold, parts of the ancient city has become flooded[79].

LOS ANGELES –

In the old Spanish Garavanza district, where Avenue 64 and York Boulevard now lie, there used to be a ranch owned by Ralph Rodgers who had employed several Mexican and Chinese workers. In early 1900 Andrew C. Smith and Charles A. Elder, discovered a rumored tunnel entrance in the area and reported it to the local newspaper, whose editor confirmed their story. They explored the tunnel to some depth. They also learned from a Mexican elder of a Native American village that existed on the banks of the Arroyo Seco River.

When the Spanish entered the area this man, Juan Dominquez, had explored the tunnel "leading to a gigantic cave and then still going further down", spreading under the entire village of Garavanza and connecting to the Spanish Church of the Angels on North Avenue.

One entrance was reportedly located along the west bluff of Arroyo Seco River about 300 feet south of the former Pasadena Ave. Rail Bridge, and about 20 feet above the stream, but the city "blew up" the entrance after

---

[79] QUEST FOR THE LOST CITY, article by Sanford M. Cleveland in AMAZING STORIES magazine, July 1947; see also THE LIZARD PEOPLE UNDER LOS ANGELES

children were hurt in the cave, and a Freeway exists now in the area, however a secret opening still exists in the basement of the Spanish church mentioned above.

Early visitors to the cave had reported "many caverns and tunnels going deep down, with eerie voices coming from them." The cave used to be used by natives for ritual purposes[80].

MOJAVE –

Stories of underground pits and shafts [some natural, others artificial mine-shafts] leading to underground caverns below Iron Canyon near the El Paso Mts. NE of Mojave. There have been reports of underground alien activity, automatons, and electromagnetic vortexes, all of which are carefully monitored by secret government agents. [see also: CALIFORNIA, EL PASO MOUNTAINS]

OAKVILLE –

Just east of Santa Rosa, there is a secret government facility that has been constructed near the Oakville Grade, which will reportedly consolidate many of the C.O.G. [Continuity Of Government] operations of the Military-Industrial Complex. Black "mystery helicopters" have been seen leaving and entering the facility on a constant basis[81].

PALMDALE –

---

[80] Article by Hank Krastman in THE HOLLOW HASSLE INSIDER, Vol.3, No.1; The Church of the Angels - Los Angeles
[81] Several issues of the NAPA SENTINEL Newspaper

There are reports of a multi-layered technology center over 8 levels in depth and the size of a massive city lying beneath Palmdale. Many of the workers are said to be "synthetics" and humans with "ultra top secret" security clearances[82].

QUINCY –

Cossette Willoughby tells about an experience that she and her husband Ken had while staying at a turnout about 20 miles from Quincy, in a heavily wooded area. She saw an "old man" with white hair, white shirt and dark trousers who "swung his head from side to side like a lizard as he walked, he had a reptilian appearance [and] carried a very elaborate cane [with] a large ball carved on top with four cobras wound around the stick." When she tried to get his attention the "man" ignored her, walking across the road from one patch of woods to another, in an area where the turnout was the closest sign of civilization for several miles around[83].

SALTON SEA –

Mountains adjacent to the Salton Sea of Southern California have been the site of reports of subterranean rock slides, and also legends concerning the ancient "seven caves" of the Aztecs which some believe lie below the area[84].

---

[82] THE PHOENIX LIBERATOR, July 7, 1992; The Skunk Works - Palmdale
[83] Cossette Willoughby of Fairacres, New Mexico; Quincy, California map
[84] Penny Harper; Salton Sea Naval facility

SAN DIEGO –

The COMTRAPAC submarine base in San Diego reportedly maintains several underground levels. The 6th sub-level is said to contain a terminal to a sub-shuttle transit system capable of subterranean hi-speed transit to other U.S. underground bases as far away as Washington D.C[85].

SAN FRANCISCO –

There is a report of a demolition crew who, several years ago, broke into a subterranean tunnel while demolishing a building in San Francisco. Workers followed the tunnel for a while until they came face to face with hairy animal-men whose eyes reflected their lights back at them with a reddish glow[86].

TEHACHAPI MTS.

[The Tehachapi Mountains, NW of Los Angeles] - Several accounts suggest that the military-industrial complex has entered in to a collaboration with a parasitical alien race. In exchange for advanced technology the industrialists have allowed the aliens to have access to the multi-trillion dollar military-industrial underground network in order to carry out "genetic experiments" on earth.

Those who received the new "Trojan horse" technology also received major alien mind-control programming, and as a result the underground networks are

---

[85] UFO JOURNAL OF FACTS, Spring, 1991 [a MUFON research journal], article by Forest Crawford of Illinois-Missouri MUFON; San Diego Sub-Base
[86] NEW ATLANTEAN JOURNAL[?]; a Related Site?

quickly being assimilated by the alien collective, effectively controlling the minds of those earth people who pose the greatest threat to alien imperialism, i.e. those who have access to interplanetary technology.

Tehachapi is also called the "Anthill", there are open silos where laser light systems are tested and hovering basket-ball sized cosmodrones or "spybees" monitor all activity above and below ground, where "ground-scrapers" descend at least 2 miles and 42 sub-levels, connecting to other facilities via tunnels and mag-lev shuttles and also to more ancient alien cavern domains [natural and artificial] deep beneath the earth.

There are also reportedly cloned humans with cybernetic minds and assimilated reptilian/alien DNA which work in these facilities known as the 'Orange' because of their 'stalky' yellowish or reddish hair, along with Grey aliens, Reptiloids, Military Industrial Black Ops, and others. This site is also known as the Tejon or Tahachapi "Ranch", and is located at the mouth of Little Oak Canyon, about 25 miles NW of Lancaster. It is partially powered by the Kern River hydroelectric project, where there is also a mountain that has been "hollowed out".

One can reportedly drive underground [with required security clearance] from California City to Palmdale to George AFB/Victorville through underground cities and tunnels where aliens have been seen "all over the place", having free access to the underground network, yet these aliens have been known to abduct or even kill some who have reported their presence there, because the aliens operate "inside our government" [via the Military-Industrial

Trojan horse which operates largely outside of Congressional oversight] and do not want their subversive activities to be discovered by the masses or by more benevolent space forces who are at war with these "regressive" alien forces.

These regressive aliens attempt to create a facade of benevolence towards those "programmed" humans who work in the underground facilities, or use fear and intimidation towards those who are aware of their true intentions. Reports of abductions and dissections of humans abound, reportedly with the purpose of "finding our weaknesses and learning how to control us" through controlling the social infrastructure upon which most have become dependent[87].

YUCCA MOUNTAIN –

Reports of underground tunnels descending several miles beneath the Yucca Mountain[88].

SANTA ROSA –

Underground FEMA facility[89] located in Santa Rosa.

MOUNT RAINIER

A very active UFO base exists beneath Mt. Rainier. There are also said to be underground "vaults" containing

---

[87] THE PHOENIX LIBERATOR, July, 1992; Val Valerian; Michael Lindemann; "High Strangeness in the Antelope Valley", by William F. Hamilton III
[88] THE PHOENIX LIBERATOR, July 7, 1992; the Los Alamos Labs - Yucca Mountain Project
[89] Richard Sauder

records of the ancient Lemurians. (Note: F.L. Boschke wrote the book "The Unexplained" about the mysteries surrounding Mt. Ranier.) The ice cap of Mt. Ranier contains a maze of corridors and caves. In August of 1970, scientists climbed to the top of Mt. Ranier, and entered these caverns and tunnels. Evidence was found indicating that a small lake exists deep beneath the ice cap. It is possible that one could find a way to get beneath Mt. Ranier through these tunnels.

The Mt. Lassen Entrance Mt. Lassen in Tehama County, California is an entrance to a large underground city. Near the foot of Mt. Lassen is a town called Manten. A man named "Ralph B. Fields" lived (lives?) there, and found the entrance to the underground city. His friend "Joe" was with him. The cave entrance is in the side of the mountain, at a little over 7,000 feet above sea level, and is near a rock outcropping suitable for camping under.

DEATH VALLEY -

Local Indian legends speak of a tunnel that runs beneath the desert. The book "Death Valley Men," tells the story of 3 people who are supposed to have found an underground city connected with this tunnel, and who actually took treasures from it. The entrance to the Death Valley Tunnel is in the Panamint Mountains down on the lower edge of the range near Wingate Pass, in the bottom of an old abandoned shaft. The bottom of the shaft is collapsed, opening an entrance into a large tunnel system containing much treasure.

These tunnels connect with the surface also through arches (like large windows) in the side of the mountain and they look down on Death Valley. They're high above the valley now, but they were once on the edge of the water, and were accessed by boats. The "windows" in the Death Valley side of the Panamint Mountains are about 4,500-5,000 feet above the bottom of Death Valley, and are across from Furnace Creek Ranch. From these openings you can see the green of the ranch below you and Furnace Creek Wash across the valley. (So, with high-powered binoculars or a telescope, you should be able to see the openings from the Furnace Creek Ranch, or Wash.)

You can drive down Emigrant Canyon towards Death Valley. You can then park beside the road between Furnace Creek Ranch and the Salt Bed. (From here, the windows should be visible through binoculars.) Indian legends of the Paiutes Indians speak of the people who used to live in the Panamint's caverns.

MOUNT SHASTA
There are tunnels beneath Mt. Shasta that lead to a UFO base there, as well as tunnels that connect with the vast world-wide tunnel network. The Lemurian city "Telos" is said to exist beneath Mt. Shasta. William Hamilton has done much research on Mt. Shasta and the tunnels. He has privately published a book entitled "Alien Magic" 249 North Brand Boulevard, Suite 651 Glendale, CA 91203

COLORADO

BLANCA PEAK –
Mt. Blanca [Massif] is located in the mysterious San Luis Valley of Colorado, which has been a "hot spot"

for UFO sightings and animal mutilations. Also Southwestern tribes have legends involving caverns below the Mt. Blanca, San Luis Lakes, and Great Sand Dunes National Monument region, through which their ancestors migrated during a time of surface natural disasters before emerging onto the surface once again. There have been some rumors of an attempted government attack upon an underground alien [Grey] base beneath Mt. Blanca, using a deadly nerve agent, which backfired or failed. Blanca peak is located between Alamosa and Walsenberg.

DELAWARE BAY –

Richard S. Shaver created a stir in AMAZING STORIES Magazine from 1945-1950 after sending a ms. to editor Ray Palmer [who backed Kenneth Arnold's investigation of the 'Maurey Island/Tacoma' UFO incident which also involved military industrialist agent Fred L. Crisman -- who later happened to be a close associate of Clay Shaw who Attorney James Garrison accused of being the Mafia-CIA go-between in the JFK assassination], Palmer also having publicized Arnold's own sighting of disc-shaped craft over Mt. Rainier, which became the original source for the term "flying saucers". Shaver's ms. was originally titled A WARNING TO FUTURE MAN, until it was embellished and "occultized" by Palmer to accommodate his metaphysical and science-fiction oriented readership, and re-named I REMEMBER LEMURIA.

Shaver told of his experiences where he would "hear peoples thoughts" while working on a certain arc welding machine at an auto plant in Detroit. The "machine" made him sensitive to the thought-waves of others in the factory, however he claimed that many of the "voices" or thought-waves what he intercepted did not come from the factory but emanated from caverns BELOW Detroit involved a warring subterranean factions known as the dero and the tero, of star-ships, machines capable of transmitting electronically-enhanced focused encephalographic or telepathic beams or rays, and other bizarre and horrific realities.

Shaver also told of how his first visit to "the caves" occurred when a "hologram" of a young woman led him to a cavern entrance; also of his second and last physical visit to a hidden cave entrance on the east coast of Delaware [Bay], via a boat by which he navigated the water-filled passage for a few miles until reaching a "Tero" city. While there the "Deros", he claimed, attacked and killed all of his Tero "friends", but for some reason they left Shaver alive. Shaver left the cave and never returned to the inner world physically, however he continued to receive "thought beams" which claimed to originate from other "Teros" yet which became increasingly occultic and confusions, suggesting, according to some, that the "Deros" were manipulating Shaver in order to bring ridicule to the subject of an underground reality that was on the verge of becoming public knowledge on the surface.

The "Shaver Mystery" DID however provoke much feedback from others who recounted similar experiences with the underground realm, however the highly occultic "messages" that Shaver continued to receive for years afterwards led many to become entangled in deeply occultic practices and belief systems and also paranoid schizophrenic behaviors. Who or whatever was manipulating Shaver's mind apparently succeeded in dragging many people under their occultic influence. According to Ray Palmer, who stayed overnight at Shaver's house on on occasion, he heard five separate and distinct voices one night coming out of Shaver, who was apparently linked to a collective mind via electro-telepathic waves.

The "group" of voices which were being channeled through Shaver were matter-of-factly discussing the murder and dismemberment of a woman within "the caves", and one of the "voices" was stating -- according to Palmer -- that such things should not be taking place[90].

FLORIDA –

MIAMI –

Beneath Miami, there is said to be an underground genetics-breeding facility with several mature and young girls being held captive by grey aliens. Used to breed a "hybrid" slave labor race that is intended to infiltrate surface society and do the bidding of the New World Order, which is to be ultimately controlled by an alien agenda[91].

GEORGIA –

Engineer Rex Ball came upon a network of tunnels in Georgia in 1940, which led to an underground installation manned by Oriental-looking men in coveralls

---

[90] AMAZING STORIES Magazine; THE HIDDEN WORLD; SHAVER MYSTERY Magazine; CAVEAT EMPTOR; SHAVERTRONmagazine; Richard Shaver, the founder of Ufology?
[91] Mr. X

and a few American military officers. When caught in the tunnels, an officer issued the curt command: "Make him look like a nut!" The next thing he recalled was waking up in a field uncertain whether the experience was real or a dream[92].

ATLANTA –

A major underground Bavarian Illuminati facility constructed in collaboration with a similar base below the Denver International Airport. Like the DIA facility, the Atlanta facility is occupied by the cult of the serpent [human & alien collaborators] and is "intended" to be used jointly with the Denver Airport facility as duel U.S. headquarters for New World Order regional control, and for continued "Montauk" or "Phoenix" Project operations[93].

DOUGLAS –

In the 1950's, Earl Meeks was drilling a well on his property 6 miles from Douglas when he broke through to empty space. The shaft began to suck in a constant flow of air and sounds resembling "an underground railway" were so loud that they had to cover the "well" with planks at night so that they could sleep. A few decades later a subscriber to THE HOLLOW EARTH INSIDER, "Lucky", visited the Meeks homestead 6 miles WEST of Douglas, and learned that people from all over the state had come to investigate the well the entire 2 weeks that it sucked in air, before the Meeks finally had it capped off. "Lucky" told of

---

[92] THE MOTHMAN PROPHECIES, by John A. Keel
[93] Mr. X

his intention to seek permission from the Meeks to uncap the well[94].

MARIETTA –

A planned underground Pentagon facility below Kennesaw Mountain, a few miles from Dobbins Air Force Base, to be used as a "defense" installation for the surrounding 13 states region, was reported by Richard Sauder[95].

THOMASVILLE –

Beneath Thomasville, there is said to be an underground FEMA facility[96].

IDAHO

BURLEY –

Druggist George Haycock claimed that he had explored a shaft that could be entered via a boulder strewn depression or sink 6 miles west of Burley, and one mile off the main road [presumably in the opposite direction from the river?]. Native American legends told of a demonic race that would emerge from a cave and capture their women and children. Mr. Haycock reported psychic attacks and impressions of evil activities taking place underground. The shaft led to a long square-cut yet ancient horizontal crawlspace tunnel with branch tunnels and a cave-in which he attempted to dig through, although experiencing unusual

---

[94] FATE Magazine, Jan. 1957; THE HOLLOW EARTH INSIDER, Vol.1, No.4 [Spring, 1993]
[95] UNDERGROUND BASES AND TUNNELS, by Richard Sauder
[96] Ibid

"resistance" in doing to. He later wrote friends that someone was trying to blast the shaft closed with dynamite and also reported a death threat he had received in the mail telling him to cease and desist his explorations. Shortly after this, he was found strangled to death in his home[97].

ILLINOIS

CHICAGO –

Allegations that the Bahai Temple near Chicago, which has foundation "pillars" reaching hundreds of feet to the bedrock below, contains an entrance to an underground system deep below which connect to other underground systems[98].

KENTUCKY

PIKEVILLE –

Strange disappearances have been reported in the Truck Coal Mine 3 miles east of Pikeville. Two boys seen entering the mine disappear even though their lamp is found abandoned at the entrance. A full scale search of the mine fails to turn up any evidence of the missing boys[99].

APPALACHIAN MOUNTAINS

Appalachian Mountains were formed when the sea closed by collision between America and Europe, they grow 45,000ft high. what we see today are the roots of the

---

[97] AMAZING STORIES magazine, Oct. 1947 & Jan. 1948
[98] Kenneth Van Hoof
[99] FATE magazine, Nov. 1950

mountains. at such high pressure, rock act as a fluid, what you talk about are frozen waves of rock.

PINEVILLE –

On Dec. 26, 1945, a mine explosion in the Belva Mine trapped several men. When they were rescued some of the men insisted that they saw a "door" in one of the walls open, and a man dressed as a "lumberjack" emerge from a well-lighted room. After assuring the men that they would be rescued, the strange visitor returned to the room and closed the door. Other similar accounts have been reported during similar mine disasters, such as the one at a Shipton, Pennsylvania mine, where similar "lumberjack" or "telephone linemen" type of men have been seen, suggesting that they exist in another time-dimension, possibly explaining why they "knew" the outcome of the disasters. In some cases the strange "workmen", as if taking the role of guardian angels, had offered trapped men unusual "lighting" to keep them out of the dark, and in other cases as with the Shipton disaster, "astral visions" accompanied the visits of these fourth dimensional [?] visitors[100].

RIVERTON –

Patsey Wingate, a victim of UFO encounters, missing time, MIB limo's, harassment, black helicopters, police-like cars in a temporal mist, death threats, the works... spoke of a mountain near Riverton where a certain UFO was seen on numerous occasions. While on the mountain she would hear humming sounds coming from

---

[100] Pineville Kentucky newspapers, circa Dec. 26, 1981 - Jan. 1982

underground, then at home later that night she experienced frightening vivid "dreams" of "children underground on the mountain [who] were begging for help. They were in glass cages. Some of the children looked human, but some looked like aliens[101]."

SALEM –

SE of Salem is Hodges cave, which some believe is the cavern that is mentioned in John Uri Lloyd's book ETIDORHPA, which was illustrated by a veteran Mason. Witnesses have stated that they have seen Masons wandering about the area. One report tells of a nearby stone staircase leading deep into the gloomy darkness of the earth, which witnesses failed to fully investigate as they were hit with an overpowering sense of terror[102].

STOVEN'S CAVE [SITE UNSPECIFIED] –

In Stoven's Cave unusual sounds emanating from the cavern[103].

TAZEWELL COUNTY –

In Tazewell County, Higgingbottom #1 or Devil's Slide cave is avoided by local residents because they are convinced that some loathsome creature lives at the bottom[104].

LOUISIANA

---

[101] UFO UNIVERSE, Vol.3, No.2, [Summer 1993]
[102] THE SHAVER MYSTERY magazine
[103] TECH TROGLODYTE [NSS affiliate newsletter], Vol.12, No.2
[104] CAVE LEGENDS OF THE APPALACHIANS, article by Janice Goad

FORT POLK –

AT FORT POLK, THERE HAVE BEEN Reports of over 19,000 war-ready United Nations Organization troops, French, Pakistani & Russian, along with massive underground facilities for storage of military and other supplies[105].

MARYLAND

CROFTON –

An ancient network of tunnels and crawlways discovered beneath a parking lot in Crofton during excavations. The artificial tunnels were reportedly covered by subsequent construction[106].

FORT MEADE –

"Cavernous subterranean expanses" existing beneath the National Security Agency's headquarters at Fort Meade are said to be, filled with over 10 acres of the most sophisticated supercomputers money can buy, which monitor global telephone, telegraph, telex, fax, radio, TV, microwave, internet and other forms of communication[107].

BETWEEN OLNEY & LAYTONSVILLE –

Located on Riggs Road, off of Rt. 108, this underground facility is maintained by FEMA [Federal Emergency Management Agency]. Long lines of cars have

---

[105] a former anonymous serviceman who interacted with the base
[106] THE WASHINGTON STAR NEWS, July 25, 1973 & Aug. 15, 1973
[107] UFO Magazine, Vol.7, No.6; Richard Sauder

been seen heading through the gate at shift change, in spite of the surface illusion of vacancy and disrepair, vehicles which pass through an electronic surveillance area and disappear behind a knoll in the near distance. At least 10 levels deep, and several electronic surveillance facilities, with possible NSA connections[108].

THURMONT - see: PENNSYLVANIA, BLUE RIDGE SUMMIT

MASSACHUSETTS

BOSTON –
Ervin M. Scott claimed to have intercepted an electronically augmented telepathic transmission from a woman, a cavern-dweller under the Salt Lake flats of Utah, whose people were under siege by the "evil ones". She urgently warned about a woman who was abducted into tunnels/caverns beneath an abby in the north section of Boston 3 weeks earlier [the 1st church of Roxbury is located in the north section of the city and is by far the oldest "abby" in Boston]. Another "voice" breaks in on the "transmission" and tells Ervin not to believe the former woman's voice, stating, "Don't you know this is a lie? a trick?", and then warningly, "keep quiet about this!"[109].

MAYNARD –
At Maynard is said to be an underground FEMA facility.

---

[108] UFO Magazine, Vol.7, No.6; Richard Sauder
[109] SEARCH magazine, July 1964

MICHIGAN

BATTLE CREEK –
At Battle Creek there is said to be an underground FEMA facility[110].

MINNESOTA

REDWOOD FALLS –
A WWII trainee claimed to have discovered a small underground passage near [west of?] Redwood Falls, which led to an ancient tiled concourse and to an underground alien realm. He spoke of the "deros" and "teros" and stated that he emerged 6 months later with a "tero" woman who became his wife, with no intention on returning, although both lived in fear as if they were constantly being watched or followed[111].

MISSOURI

CAMERON –
At Cameron thee are rumors of a "haunted" cave or mine in the area

KANSAS CITY –
Somewhere on the Missouri river near Kansas City a man explored a cave in the side of a steep embankment on somewhere on the rivers edge. He was terrified by a tall

---

[110] Richard Sauder
[111] letter sent to Richard Shaver [circa 1950's]

creature with cat or lizard like eyes, who had apparently been living in the cave or possibly had come from the river itself[112].

CARTHAGE

BUFO Paranormal and UFO Radio
Incident Date: March 7, 2004 - Carthage Missouri.

     This past Sunday...the 7th. A friend and I were riding two ATVs in a place called, "The Underground" it is a public and private storage facility in Carthage, Mo. What makes this place such a desirable storage facility is that it is all underground...hence the name. They are constantly expanding this place and there are miles and miles of carved out caves in there...and it goes pretty deep. This facility stores thousands and thousands of food containers, all dehydrated for the Navy... I have seen them and it is public knowledge around here. It is also a fall out shelter able to hold some 40,000 to 50,000 people. I tell you this to give some sense of the vastness of the place. I worked there as a subcontractor some 9 years ago... I helped build the office spaces up on top. I started to explore then... about once a month and did so all the way until this past Sunday. However, I never went as far or as deep before either.

     It was fun to take the ATVs and cruise underground...no rain or weather problems...ever. We were approx 8 miles in and I'd say maybe 500 feet deep when we took a turn down an area that was marked "Naval Authoritative Zone" I remember making a comment about the Navy getting a ship down there and said that was an

---

[112] Charles Marcoux

easy posting. The walls became more defined as in: polished or finished and this was striking because this was supposed to be a newly blasted area... totally backward I would think...still thinking nothing was wrong we kept going, actually increasing speed because the floor was paved now and we could go faster.

We came up on an unusual painted pattern on the floor and I thought, "cool graffiti... kids have been down here... we're safe... won't get into any trouble." The road dipped down and then it took a 90' turn to the left... we had no warning and we were going too fast. I knew we were going to hit the wall. BUT we DIDN'T... we passed through some kind of projection of the cave siding... although I don't know how it was done...it was real looking. We passed into a whole new road system... this one was large, and much older than where we came from.

We started to smell an odor...musty, damp, growing stronger as we went deeper on smell. The lighting decreased as well probably 60% less than the other area's...we turned on our headlights. We continued on at about 5 to 7 miles an hour for about 5 min and we noticed it was getting cooler... which was to me, very strange...since once inside a cave a certain distance... the temp says the same. We made a right turn and started to come up on what I thought was a rest area on the side... about 40 feet away.

I thought it looked like a pair of fountains until they moved. We both stopped immediately. We were approx. 30' feet away now and what we saw were two creatures, one was very tall at least 7' feet maybe more and very powerfully built... reddish in color and the other was smaller about 6' feet but it was not red in color but pale, like an albino and it was not as powerfully built as the other. They looked like REPTILES... living, walking, intelligent beings... not human... not warm blooded. Reptiles! I know it sounds crazy but it is true.

They said nothing but I did get a strong sense from the big one. A malevolence, evil presence of some kind. My friend screamed and we turned around...a power turn. We started to go back out when my friend said, "the big one" was after us. I looked back and it was following us. I had the overwhelming feeling that if it caught us that harm would come to us. We passed through the wall projection and I looked back and saw the thing raise it's arm and it had a weapon of some sorts. It fired and hit the ATV my friend was on. The engine died and he stopped. I told him to jump on...and he did. I gunned it and then my friend said, "STOP!" I slowed down and he he said, "LOOK!".

I looked back and the thing had stopped at the graffiti on the cave floor/road. The ATV was on it's side of the graffiti/symbol. It was obvious the thing would not cross the marking. I slowed more...we were now about 75' feet away. I stopped and the three of us... Me, my friend and the creature/reptile/man thing just looked at each other... for about 15 sec. And let me tell you... that is a long time. Then I started to leave... It stayed there waiting and not moving until we were out of sight. As soon as we cleared the cave I got on my cell phone and called the Sheriff's Dept. I was told that they would not come out and that "Underground Security" would handle it.

Then they hung up! By law they are not to do that...We can hang up on anyone...but a government office, be it City or Federal can not hang up on you. Anyway, I was shocked and scared and we took off across the outside of the underground over to my truck and sure enough...Underground Security was waiting for us. We were told to leave, not to tell anybody about this...that if I come back...The Navy would press charges.

I was also told that I had 10 min to leave or I would be taken in. What can I say... we left. It has been 3 days since this has happened and I am still shaken. I am a powerful person, 6'4" and 265 lbs and I have never in my life be afraid for my life... until this past Sunday. I lost my one of my two ATV's. As far as I know... it is still down there. My friend will not talk about it and I have not heard anything from anyone about it. I did call the Sheriff's Dept. and they said they never got a call from me. Well, that is my story... I have never had anything strange happen in my life and I am very very concerned about this.

I can tell you this...I had an urge to kill the things I saw down there... I don't know if that is a natural reaction as most people have a natural revulsion towards reptiles or because of my faith and the feeling of evil I had... or what. All I know is that they are real...and I wish I could do something... anything to combat or help against these things. Take care all and thank you again for letting me write this and share this experience.

NEVADA-ARIZONA

Hoover Dam. Lake Mead's Hoover Dam SE of Las Vegas. Rumors that the dam construction workers penetrated extensive caverns near the base of the cliffs, that Lake Mead is a hot spot of alien activity, and that the floor of one level of the dam contains a "wild tile inlay on the floor, with signs of the zodiac and all sorts of stuff suggesting an entrance[113]."

NEVADA

BOULDER DAME –

Reports of underground tunnels and UFO activity between the base of Boulder Dam and Jumbo Peak[114].

EUREKA –

A mysterious maze of underground tunnels and rooms discovered beneath the immediate area of Eureka[115].

MERCURY –

An electrician at the Mercury Base Camp on the Nevada Test Site claimed to have seen "aliens" in "stainless steel caverns" about 3000 feet below the surface of the Mercury Site. The "Mercury Workers" contracted through Reynolds Electric [a division of E.G.&G.], and several of them told terrifying stories of harassment and death threats from base personnel in an effort to keep them from talking. Also Las Vegan Stayce Borland and her brother were killed by "burglars" during a time when they were trying to help some of the Mercury Workers who had been apprehended and were being held captive underground.

---

[113] Letter from Vaughn M. Green in SHAVERTRON newsletter, No. 14
[114] Lew Tery
[115] An Underground Cathedral", article by Charles Hillinger in THE LOS ANGELES TIMES, Mar. 2, 1975

Many insisted that Borland's murder was part of a conspiracy, similar to the 5 people killed in a "helicopter crash" some years ago who, according to former Wackenhut employee Michael Riconosciuto, were trying to escape with documentation of genetic research atrocities, alien interaction, and antigravity craft technology in the underground facilities there. This conspiracy of concealment is reportedly being run by the aliens themselves to maintain control of those military-industrial-intelligence agencies which have been infiltrated and assimilated through advanced mind control technology[116].

NEVADA CITY –

The Mayflower mine east of Nevada City contained a long tunnel from which strange noises often known to emerge, and also reports of "devils" being sighted in the nearby Murchie mine[117].

PAHRUMP –

NW of Pahrump [which lies due west from Las Vegas] is Devil's Hole National Monument, an annex of Death Valley National Monument. It is an apparently "bottomless" aqua-cave containing a species of cave fish located no where else in the world. Like the legendary "subterranean grand canyon" -- which reportedly runs beneath the Kokoweef and Dorr Peaks near the SW flank of the Ivanpah Mts. just south of highway 91 and NW of Needles, California -- the Devil's Hole water level ALSO

---

[116] "The Billy Goodman Happening" - KVEG Radia 840 AM, Las Vegas, Nevada, Nov. 19, 1989, etc.
[117] : Article by Wayland D.
Hand in CALIFORNIA FOLKLORE QUARTERLY, April, 1942

reportedly rises and falls with the tide, suggesting a connection with a massive underground sea below and upstream, possibly in the area of eastern Nevada and western Utah.

At least 2 boys disappeared trying to explore Devil's Hole, and Navy scuba divers were lowered on cables and reported seeing a large subterranean river which roared up from below, flowed across a wide expanse although they could not estimate the depth because of a myriad of colonnades of black rock through which the river flowed, before plunging once again down an abyss. This reportedly occurred in a cave NEAR Devil's Hole. Although "fenced in", Devil's Hole is open for public view[118].

RENO –

Beneath Reno is said to be an underground 'Nazi' antigravity disc facility tied-in with the Antarctica scenario[119].

NEW JERSEY

NORTHERN –

John Keel, after hearing reports of strange sounds of pulsating machines coming from caves in the mountains of northern New Jersey, personally visited some of the

BROOKHAVEN –
see: New Jersey, Newark

---

[118] ADVENTURE IS UNDERGROUND, by William Halliday; Virginia Louis Swanson
[119] Al Bielek

NEWARK –

Massive German [Thule Society] infiltration of the American military-industrial complex following WWII, via the NSA, I.T.T., ARCO, EXXON, etc., led to the construction of massive joint alien-fascist underground complexes [stemming from the Nazi alliance with an alien collaboration, based under the Gizeh plateau of Egypt - via the Grant Orient Lodge of Egyptian Freemasonry and the various Gnostic Bavarian cults that were brought back from Egypt during the Egyptian occupation of the armies of the so-called "Holy Roman Empire" Italy-Austria-Germany].

Tunnel systems run from the I.T.T. Corporation building in Newark to the I.T.T. facility at Nutley, to Wright-Patterson Air Force Base in Ohio [mag-lev tubes], to A.I.L., to Long Island [Montauk Point][120].

NUTLEY –
see: NEW JERSEY, NEWARK

PARAMUS –

A massive underground facility with an entrance located in an office building at 140 Century Road near Paramus. The building next door at 120 century road is also owned by the same company which finances projects carried out below, which deal mainly with abducted women and young girls who are heavily mind controlled using brainwashing and extreme sexual abuse and torture induced MPD alternate programmed personalities, in order to create

---

[120] ORION BASED TECHNOLOGY, MIND CONTROL AND OTHER SECRET PROJECTS, by Val Valerian

"sex agents" for a Nazi cabal which had infiltrated the American Industrial Complex following WWII. These agents are used to extract important information from, to bribe, or to blackmail powerful men. There also may be a connection to the ARCO scenario in New Jersey as well[121].

NEW MEXICO

ALBUQUERQUE –

Manzano Mountain, or the Kirtland [AFB] Munitions Storage Complex, was excavated by the Air Force to serve as a nuclear weapons storage area. The mountain is visible a couple of miles south of I-40 on the eastern outskirts of Albuquerque. Security is extremely tight. Also, reports of grey aliens operating within some of the deeper levels. A 285,000 sq. ft. underground extension facility was constructed in the same area in 1989, although heavy secrecy surrounds these facilities[122].

DULCE. –

The Jicarilla Apache Indians believe that their ancestors emerged from the caverns in ancient times. When they emerged they were plagued by monsters [saurians?]. Some wanted to go back down but once their hero's slew all of the monsters, all was at peace [ironically the Dulce underground network is now reportedly under the control

---

[121] : Mr. X
[122] UFO Magazine, Vol.7, No.6; Richard Sauder

of some of the very 'monsters' or 'reptilians' that they may have succeeded in driving underground][123].

DULCE [JICARILLA APACHE RESERVATION] –

In the town of Dulce in NW New Mexico, one block from the PAN AM building is the old high school, now used as an engineering facility by MAKEN & HANGER [originally ZIA Corp.]. Inside the facility is an elevator that leads to Level-1 of the massive underground facility beneath the Dulce area which is also known as "Ultra" or "Section-D", which runs under main street at a depth of about 200 feet.

This level is guarded by PROFORCE Security, whereas deeper and more secure levels under the Archuleta mesa to the north contain automatic devices designed to KILL intruders. Dulce is by far the most massive and most strategic of all of the underground "hubs" of the joint military-industrial / alien imperial collaboration in North America, with numerous tube-tunnels radiating to all parts of the continent and beyond[124].

DULCE, NEW MEXICO BASE

An underground Military Base/Laboratory in Dulce, New Mexico connects with the underground network of tunnels which honeycombs our planet, and the lower levels of this base are allegedly under the control of Inner Earth beings or Aliens. This base is connected to Los Alamos research facilities via an underground "tube-shuttle." (It can

---

[123] MYTHS & TALES OF THE JICARILLA APACHE INDIANS, by Morris E. Opler
[124] ALIEN MAGIC, by William F. Hamilton; The Dulce Book; Map of Dulce, New Mexico

be assumed that such a shuttle way would be a straight-line construction. It should then be possible, by using maps and some deduction, to determine the most likely location of this base, especially since the general location is already known.)

Beginning in 1947, a road was built near the Dulce Base, under the cover of a lumber company. No lumber was ever hauled, and the road was later destroyed. Navajo Dam is the Dulce Base's main source of power, though a second source is in El Vado (which is also another entrance). (Note: The above facts should also help to locate the base.) Most of the lakes near Dulce were made via government grants "for" the Indians. (Note: The September, 1983 issue of Omni (Pg. 80) has a color drawing of 'The Subterrene' - the Los Alamos nuclear-powered tunnel machine that burrows through the rock, deep underground, by heating whatever stone it encounters into molten rock, which cools after the Subterrene has moved on. The result is a tunnel with a smooth, glazing lining.)"

Bechtel (BECK-tul) is a super secret international corporate octopus, founded in 1898. Some say the firm is really a 'Shadow Government's working arm of the CIA. It is the largest Construction and Engineering outfit in the U.S.A and the World (and some say, beyond). "The most important posts in U.S.A. Government are held by former Bechtel Officers. There are over 100 Secret Exits near and around Dulce. Many around Archuleta Mesa, others to the source around Dulce Lake and even as far east as Lindrich. Deep sections of the Complex connect into natural Cavern Systems. (Note: The elevators, lights, and doors at Dulce

Base are all magnetically controlled.) The area around Dulce has had a high number of reported Animal Mutilations."

The researchers at Dulce Base have also abducted several people from Dulce's civilian population and implanted devices of various types in their heads and bodies. (Note: Livermore Berkeley Labs (where?) began producing blood for the Dulce Base in the mid 1980s, and Human and Animal abductions slowed considerably. It may be worthwhile to check-out Livermore Berkeley Labs.) DELTA group (from the National Recon Group) is responsible for security of all Alien-connected projects.

The DELTA symbol is a Black Triangle on a Red Background. Dulce Base's symbol is a Delta (triangle) with the Greek Letter "Tau" (t) within it, and then the entire symbol is inverted, so the triangle points down, and the "Tau" is also inverted. Christa Tilton (was abducted and taken to Dulce Base) She is the editor of "Crux" magazine, which deals with UFOs, abductions, etc. P.O. Box 906237 Tulsa, Oklahoma.

GUADELLUPE MTS. –

In the 1800's, two trappers reportedly discovered a cave in the Guadellupe Mts., which they followed to a considerable depth. Hiding behind a large outcropping of rock they observed in fascination and horror a procession of beings in dark hooded robes enter a large cavern and began to chant, at which a "crystal like" entity descended from the stalactites above, hovered and in a multi-colored display communicated with the beings in some type of xylophone-like manner, until it once again ascended and was lost among the stalactites above, at which the procession descended DOWNWARD through the passage from which they had emerged[125].

LOS ALAMOS –

Massive underground joint military-alien facilities at Los Alamos Labs are connected via shuttle to the Dulce, New Mexico facility to the NW. The deeper facilities under Los Alamos reportedly descend to great depths and intersect with alien sectors which constitute the largest concentration of grey alien activity in North America, with Dulce running a close second... although many of the aliens apparently commute between Dulce and Los Alamos. To minimize cattle mutilations the U.S. government has reportedly been transporting daily shipments of cattle to rendezvous points in the mountains SE of Los Alamos, where some have reported massive UFO activity on these occasions, and also ancient heiroglyphs depicting alien beings[126].

ORGAN MTS. –

60 miles NW of El Paso, Texas in the Organ Mts. of New Mexico. Helen Compton Gordon and her husband discovered an old abandoned mine far above the "Bean Blossom Mine" near their former home. Climbing the ore-splattered slope they entered the other mine and discovered deep inside an immense chasm separated from the main tunnel passage by a rock wall, on the other side of which was a narrow ledge-precipice at the edge of the chasm.

---

[125] : SHAVERTRON Magazine
[126] Thomas Costallo; Sharula [Bonnie] Dux; K. Studstrup; etc.

They threw lighted sticks down the shaft and they seemed to "fall forever", also rocks were thrown in which they could not hear hit bottom. An old timer in the area told them it was a "glory hole" and that miners tended to avoid them[127].

PIE TOWN –

An unexplored cave with large steps leading deep into the earth near El Moro National Monument NE of Pie Town. Also reports of a southern extension base between Pie Town and Datil which is linked underground to the Dulce base in NW New Mexico[128].

SAN CRISTOBAL –

A homeless man spent the night in a black rock cavern near some [hot?] springs north of San Cristobal [north of Taos]. He was frightened from the cave after seeing a "lizard like" humanoid, the size of a man and walking upright on two feet[129].

TAOS –

Reports of a native American legend stating that Montezuma was born near Taos and was "instructed by beings who lived in Pueblo Peak, which is near Blue Lake, where UFO's have been seen entering and exiting the water. Near Taos, in a cave above the Lucero River, not far from Frijoles Canyon, ancient and modern sacrifices were carried out by secret cults. "Members of secret society

---

[127] SHAVER MYSTERY magazine, Vol.1, No.2 [1947]
[128] THE HIDDEN CITY OF CHIHUATLAN, by Charles A. Marcoux; Thomas A. Castello
[129] Tim Ore

groups in Taos have been found beheaded, like Arthur Manby who told of a secret "Aztland" Hot Springs roughly 11 miles NW of Taos, flanked by petroglyphs on the canyon walls[130].

TRUTH OR CONSEQUENCES –

A Mr. Lemon stated that when he was young, about 12, he was out hunting deer NORTH of Truth or Consequences, and was tracking a wounded deer he had shot when he came across an intricately carved stone stairway that led down into the earth, which he determined to investigate after he killed the deer. He searched for years but was never able to find the enigmatic staircase again[131].

NEW YORK

MANHATTAN –

A large triangular system of tunnels utilized by a "masonic lodge", deep below the surface of Manhattan[132].

Con Edison, while drilling a test hole in the north end of East River Park, broke through to open space about 200 feet below, suggesting the existence of a large cavern below.

Strange stories of several sub-basement levels descending below the Empire State Building, rumors of descending sub-basements connecting with ancient tunnels and sub-basement levels controlled by the Federal

---

[130] ALIEN INVADERS, article/treatise by TAL LeVesque

[131] Cossette Willoughby

[132] "Tunnels and Caverns Beneath New York City", article by R. L. Blain-Sanders in the Fall, 1981 issue of SHAVERTRON Magazine

government. Following the Twin Towers bombing it was reported that 6 sub-levels controlled by the Secret Service were damaged. Also in a similar fashion LOCAL reporters in the early hours of the Oklahoma City bombing reported that underground tunnels containing all kinds of military hardware had been blasted open, and also rumors of an 18-leveled underground facility below the Murah Federal Building, with the 5 upper levels being used for parking. These aspects of the bombings were, predictably, not advertised by the national media monopolies[133]. The Episcopal Church of St. John the Divine at 103 St. and Amsterdam reportedly conceals the entrance to an underground cavern used by an occult lodge, an actual "city" left over from former sub-inhabitants of the eastern seaboard during antediluvian/Atlantean times, and protected by "space-warping" technology[134].

LINCOLN TUNNEL –

A man and his wife, traveling through winter snow, parked their car in the Lincoln tunnel to wipe the snow from off of the car, and vanished without a trace[135].

MONTAUK –

An underground base 8-9 levels deep below Camp Hero at Montauk Point, Long Island, which is reportedly occupied by Ciakars from Alpha Draco, Greys from Rigel Orion, Black Ops & German Intelligence - Thule Society agents. The Montauk mind control and space-time

---

[133] THE PHOENIX LIBERATOR; various private news sources
[134] ENCYCLOPEDIA OF OCCULTISM & PARAPSYCHOLOGY, by Leslie A. Shepard, pp. 889-890; Maurice Doreal
[135] John Grant

manipulation projects were based there and at 25 other bases around North America and reportedly involved over 25 thousand "abductees" who have been programmed to serve the as "sleeper" agents of the New World Order.

The computer archives of the Montauk Project are housed in the underground facility near the Alsace-Lorraine region near the German-French border, and is known as the Montauk Alsace Lorraine Time Archives [M.A.L.T.A.]. Entrances reportedly exist under the old 7-story Montauk Tower in the nearby town of Montauk; near the Sage Radar Tower and buildings to the north; under the old Montauk Air Force Station; Block Island; East Hampton; in a hill near the Light House at Montauk 'Point' itself; in the cliffs overlooking the beaches near Camp Hero; behind the so-called "cement bunkers" that have been sealed; under the "mystery closets" which can be seen throughout the area; and connecting the basements of three [?] buildings - now demolished - in the Shadmoor area directly west of the Ditch Plains public bathhouse and parking lot; an entrance near a boulder which sits along the west side of the SE entry road to the base; and also at Fort Pond Bay[136].

ROME –

A very large underground facility located at the Rome National Air Base where is located a "Montauk Chair" similar to the one at the base under Montauk Point, Long Island. An underground tunnel with electric cars reportedly connects this facility with another smaller facility in Rochester, an entrance to this tunnel connection

---

[136] Preston Nicholes; Peter Moon; Duncan Cameron; Al Bielek; John Quinn; Michelle Guerin; Michael Ash; Mr. "X"; etc.

allegedly being located under the Andrews Street bridge in Rochester[137].

NORTH CAROLINA

BROWN MOUNTAIN

Brown Mountain is in North Carolina near Morganton. Morganton is "about 15 miles north of an actual highway marker which has been posted by the state providing any visitor the best view" of Brown Mountain. Brown Mountain is an area in which many strange lights have been seen. There are entrances that lead inside the mountain to an isolated (?) Alien base.

OHIO

WRIGHT-PATTERSON AFB –
see: NEW JERSEY, NEWARK

OKLAHOMA

ADA –

At Ada is said to be a joint alien-military underground facility[138].

BINGER –

A large mound north of Binger has traditionally been "haunted" and also the site of a legendary entrance to a vast system of labyrinths leading to the "Land of Kenyon"

---

[137] Mr. X
[138] UFO Magazine, Vol.7, No.6, 1992

within a vast cavern illuminated by a bluish electromagnetic aurora/phosphorescence, in which live a peaceable race. However deep below this cavern are other darker realms where malevolent "serpent people" dwell[139].

MCALESTER –

Just before the Korean War three men explored a cavern NE of McAlester, underneath a "haunted mound", near which strange manifestations, animal mutilations and missing livestock had been reported. The owner at the time had put crosses on the knoll in order to keep "evil spirits" away. The three man, once inside, made their way down into a large cavern and found a seemingly "bottomless shaft" around which spiraled a stone staircase with steps large enough to accommodate a 12 foot giant. They descended for about a mile, not reaching the bottom, and decided to go back up. After the first two had emerged they heard a scream from the third, and some shots from his .45 revolver. They helped him out and in terror he told of hairy animal-men who had suddenly snuck up from behind him, grabbing him and trying to pounce him down to the ground. As evidence he showed his friends the YELLOWISH BLOOD that his gun had extracted from the creatures[140].

OKLAHOMA CITY –

Reports which surfaced in the first hours after the Oklahoma City Federal building bombing but were suppressed by the national media, of Firefighters who told of huge tunnels that had been blasted open where they were

---

[139] Charles Marcoux
[140] Charles Marcoux; Victor John C. Johnson

shocked to see huge underground rooms filled with military arsenals, including missiles and missile launchers, tanks, etc. Also reports of an 18-level base beneath this Federal Building [and others?], with the top 5 levels being used for underground parking[141].

OREGON

FORT ROCK BASIN –

Water wells north of Fort Rock Basin have been known to blow air for days during periods of high barometric pressure - times when they should rather be taking in air[142].

PORTLAND –

"The Astounding Woodstock Mystery Hole just 2 miles west of I-205 located in Portland Oregon. Inside the Mystery Hole you'll find a Giant Double Arch, Geometric "codes" inscribed on walls, and other oddities. A Black Obsidian Mirror, and a Florite Crystal Tower, reconstructed based on information gleaned from the curious glyphs sculptured on the Giant Double Arch found deep inside The Mystery Hole[143]."

PENNSYLVANIA

ALLEGHENY MOUNTAINS –

---

[141] THE PHOENIX LIBERATOR
[142] "Central Oregon's Underground World Filled With Wind That Roars, Whistles...", Article by Larry Chitwood in THE OREGONIAN, Oct. 31, 1985
[143] INSIDE THE MYSTERY HOLE website

About 50 miles south of Pittsburgh in the first range of the Allegheny mountains, George A. Lehew reportedly found a cavern which he penetrated for over a mile, the passages becoming increasingly wider. He descended at about a 45 degree angle until reaching a room in which he found a 6-ft.-wide thermal bore, a perfectly circular shaft with smooth glazed walls that had apparently been melted through the rock/earth in some ancient time.

Old timers in the area alleged that six "survivors" in 1915 took gear and equipment and spent a month exploring the cave, going 18 miles from the entrance and down almost 5 miles below sea level, where they distinctly heard the "rumble of machinery" off in the distance[144].

BLUE RIDGE SUMMIT –

The location of the so-called "underground Pentagon" maintained by nearby Ft. Ritchie, and used as a major electronic nerve center for the U.S. military. A massive installation that is also known as "Raven Rock" or "Site R" that was blasted out of greenstone granite 650 feet below. A 260,000 sq. ft. facility sprawling beneath 716 acres composed of five different "buildings" in specially excavated separate caverns, literally forming an underground "pentagon".

Also contains fluorescent lights, convenience store, barbershop, medical and dining facilities, an underground reservoir containing millions of gallons of water, a chapel, 35 miles of telephone lines, and six 1,000-watt generators. It is a supercomputing and electronic command post linked

---

[144] Letter from George A. Lehew in AMAZING STORIES Magazine, Dec. 1946

with several military communications networks around the globe, and is reportedly connected via tunnel to Camp David several miles to the north near the town of Thurmont[145].

DIXONVILLE –

Mine inspector Glenn E. Berger reported in 1944 to his superiors that the Dixonville mine disaster which "killed" 15 men was not the result of a cave-in, but rather an attack by underground creatures capable of manipulating the earth [partial cave-ins], whose domain the miners had apparently penetrated.

Most of the dead miners were not injured by falling rocks but showed signs of large claw marks, others were missing, and one survivor spoke of seeing a vicious humanoid creature that was 'not of this world' within an ancient passage that the miners had broken into. The creature somehow created a "cave-in", blocking himself and another inspector [who closed his eyes when he felt the creatures 'hot breath' on his neck] from the main passage until another rescue party began to dig through the collapse, scaring the "creature" away.[146]

NEW KENSINGTON –

A creature, about 4 ft. tall, walking on two feet and "half humanoid - half dinosaur" was seen by grownups and children near New Kensington. One boy attempted to grab the creature from behind, which let out a squealing or screeching sound and escaped. Also, children attempted to

---

[145] UFO Magazine, Vol.7, No.6; Richard Sauder
[146] Article by Stoney Brakefield in NEWS EXTRA, July 14, 1974

pour gasoline on the creature and light it, unsuccessfully, before it escaped into a "sewer tunnel" nearby[147].

PITTSBURGH –

Two boys enter a cave in a Pittsburgh suburb that was uncovered by road excavation work, only to find a partially buried thermal-bore [a perfectly round fused polished shaft apparently melted through the rock], partially concealed by dirt, and which they uncover and explore. Their dog runs down the sloping shaft, which is about 4 ft. in diameter, ahead of them until a deep, vibrating sound is heard, following which the dog came running back out of the shaft, clawing its way over them and in total terror, running back home.

The cave was then subsequently covered by further road excavation. Also rumors of old robber gangs in frontier times who would rob banks and escape to hide away in ancient caverns underground, via an "automatic door" they had discovered in the cliffs[148].

SOUTH CAROLINA

COLUMBIA –

The alleged discovery of an underground tunnel by a family picnicking in the suburban town of Irmo, 4 miles NW of Columbia, Irmo having been suspected in the past of harboring U.N. fugitives. John Don Cooper and his son

---

[147] "Green Thing Sparks Rumors", article by Michael Burke, in THE VALLEY NEWS DISPATCH, New Kensington-Terentum & Vandergraft, PA., March 5, 1981 issue
[148] THE SHAVER MYSTERY Magazine

Wayne Dwayne discovered the opening while out foraging for branches for their makeshift lean-to. The passage led to a man-made cave. According to police spokesman Ralph Hightower the tunnel was located in a wooded area next to the parking lot of the Irmo K-Mart, which was not heavily visited due to competition from a nearby Wal-Mart and Sam's Club.

Cooper immediately called 1-1-1 and the Irmo SWAT Team responded by storming K-Mart and the tunnel. Caught by surprise, the U.N. infiltrators lost the battle, which lasted about 4 hours, however it was found that the tunnel branched out to many different and still unknown locations. The tunnel at the town limits of Irmo was sealed by the SWAT Team. Hightower said: "...I don't think they'll be back 'cause we kicked their butts real good[149]."

GAFFNEY –

In the mid-1960's, a woman in Gaffney complained to the local police that someone was digging tunnels under her house, as she was plagued by eerie hums and strange mechanical sounds emanating from under her house[150].

TENNESSEE

GALLATIN –

On Sept. 23, 1880 at about 3:30 in the afternoon near the town of Gallatin, farmer David Land dematerialized in front of 5 witnesses while walking across

---

[149] local newspaper article from Columbia, S.C., Nov. 23, 1997
[150] : THE 8TH TOWER, by John A. Keel

a field. Mrs. Lang ran and pounded the ground where he had vanished. Seven months later Lang's children insisted that they had heard their father crying distantly from UNDERNEATH the field. He seemed desperate and tortured, and was begging for help, until his voice faded away and was not heard again. Where he was last seen there was a circle of WITHERED yellow grass 20 feet in diameter[151].

TEXAS

ALPINE –

The 'haunted' Refugio mine in the Chispa Mts. 60 miles SW of Alpine, which had been abandoned in spite of a large amount of silver ore still remaining within. As one investigator attempted to enter a 'drift', a thunderous noise and a rush of air came from the tunnel, throwing him against the opposite wall, bruised and dazed, as the air subsided "one of the post piercing and plaintive cries I ever heard" emerged, the terrorized Henry Boyd said. The phenomena was repeated as he left the mine, and later attempts to work the mine ended in injury and terror, some of the men who later attempted to enter the enigmatic tunnel were thrown repeatedly broken and bruised against the tunnel walls as if by an invisible force[152].

ATHENS –

---

[151] MAJESTIC, by Whitley Streiber
[152] NEW YORK HERALD, Jan. 4, 1903

Near Athens is said to be a Joint alien-military underground facility[153].

BETWEEN FREDRICKSBURG & MASON –

Kiser cave reportedly pours out a steady stream of carbon dioxide from its mouth, a phenomena which has not yet been explained[154].

DALLAS –

The Texas Instruments plant, near the main gate of the Dallas facility, allegedly conceals an underground entrance leading to large caverns below. Allegations that certain "Shaver Mystery" experts were asked to enter the caverns where small green-skinned humanoids were being contained in cages, in order to offer their opinions as to who or what the beings were[155].

DENTON –

Near Denton is an underground FEMA facility[156].

EL PASO –

There is a tunnel in the Franklin Mountains above El Paso that is said to enter the Aztec underworld said to exist in a massive cavern complex beneath New Mexico. At this point there are no further details[157].

There is also evidence that there is a tunnel complex of more than 900 miles extending from beneath El Paso

---

[153] UFO Magazine, Vol.7, No.6, 1992
[154] EXPLORING AMERICAN CAVES, by Franklin Folsom
[155] Henry M. Steele
[156] Richard Sauder
[157] THE HIDDEN CITY OF CHIHUATLAN, by Charles A. Marcoux

that runs deep into Mexico, as far east as Horizon city, Texas and as far west as Las Vegas, New Mexico and far to the north[158].

FORT WORTH –

On the afternoon of Friday, July 13th, 1984, a 20 foot long, 2-foot-high bulge stretched the surface of a street in Fort Worth as if a giant earthworm was trying to come up from under the road. It seemed alive, swaying back and forth, said Charlie McCafferty of the fire dept. "What spooked me was there wasn't even a crack in the road." Jackhammers were used to break through the asphalt & concrete, where they found silt layers intact and no evidence of gas buildup. Shortly after the above event a similar mound was seen on Calvin Lang's homestead at the outskirts of Ft. Worth, and after prodding it with a rake it disappeared yet it had left some buildings torn apart, fences torn down, and shrubs and trees uprooted.

Later Jeremy Boiter spotted what appeared to be a giant tentacle erupting from the ground in a shower of gravel and dirt about 2 miles away. It seized a can and her kittens, devouring them in seconds as well as two growling dog which it swallowed in its "slick dripping mouth". His friend Phil Dewar also found scraps of birds, rabbits and other while animals among the rubble of a destroyed hut[159].

UTAH-ARIZONA –

---

[158] Hudnall, Ken and Sharon Hudnall, El Paso: A City of Secrets, Omega Press, El Paso, TX.
[159] THE WORLD'S MOST INCREDIBLE STORIES, by Adam Sisman; THE GAZETTE, Schenectady, N.Y., 16 July 1984; NATIONAL EXAMINER, 12 Feb. 1985

"A-K warriors watching undercover and very secretive government movements going on in southern Utah and northern Arizona by the government and archaeology dept. of Utah. They are mapping the Anasazi underground caverns and tunnel systems in Arizona, Utah, Nevada, and New Mexico. This action has been going on for about 2 years. They are using a new development of radar coupled with seismographic signals. One of ours spies in the government said recently that they have made some rather astounding discoveries. Navaho and Kaweah warriors are watching this gab gang of white men. Kawewah warriors in Arizona are looking for two gold hunters in south Arizona area[160]."

UTAH

ALPINE –

This "suburban legend" involves a farmer near Alpine who solicited the help of some other men to move a large boulder in his field. The boulder was moved, only to reveal a tunnel leading downward. They descended the sloping tunnel but came to a place where their progress was prevented by a "giant serpent". In fear, they went back to the surface and re-sealed the shaft with the boulder[161].

CANYON-LANDS NATIONAL PARK –

---

[160] "Anasazi Underground", report from AMERICAN INDIAN DEFENSE, Hutchinson, Kansas
[161] K. Studstrup

The Druid Arch area is reportedly the site of a joint alien-military base. Many unusual phenomena have been described, including strange men "posing" as park rangers discouraging people from going into certain "public" areas, invisible military personnel who could only been seen as reflections in mirrors, UFO sightings and manifestations, and also a high level of electromagnetic energy which adversely affects electronic equipment[162].

DUGWAY –

Reported underground connection to the Sub-Global network, and also reports of automatons and reptilian humanoids operating under holographic human disguises, who have been seen to transform temporarily to their alien state, according to a hair stylist and a worker at an auto shop in the town of Dugway who both witnesses such temporary transformations.

LITTLE COTTONWOOD CANYON –

A few miles up Little Cottonwood Canyon there are 3 switch backs on the north side of the road, with security signs posted, leading up to the "granite" cliffs. The first switch back leads to the underground records vault maintained by the Mormon church, which has an underground but "off limits" connecting passage which leads deeper into the mountain, to a massive cavern where military and alien personnel collaborate, and in which witnesses have observed massive construction projects, and large underground buildings in which humans and greys

---

[162] "Lands of Ancient Star People", article by Robert Morning Sky in UFO UNIVERSE, Spring, 1996

have been seen working at benches on electronic [mind control, etc.] equipment.

Also, reports of a "Melchizedek" lodge penetrating the Mormon/LDS and Masonic lodges, the Mt. Shasta Mayan colony, and other 'lodges' in Sirius and Arcturus, which have formerly maintained treaties with the grey aliens although many of them have turned against the greys as a result of their betrayals of interactive treaties. The 2nd and 3rd switch backs going up the canyon both intersect at the same point, which is apparently the main surface entrance to the underground "military" facility.

SALEM-THISTLE –

Under the mountains between Salem and Thistle [ghost town] Utah, there are, according to reports, caverns in which a joint Nazi - Masonic - Reptilian underground facility is maintained. Also reports of massive alien/reptilian "infiltration" activity in the area and especially along the "Wasatch Front" of the Western Rockies.

SALT LAKE CITY AIRPORT –

Beneath the Salt Lake City Airport is said to be an underground FEMA facility[163].

SALT LAKE CITY –

Massive underground facility for human cloning, beneath the University of Utah, where human cloning has been carried out at least since 1977[164].

---

[163] Alan DeWalton

Below Crossroads Plaza [via the EXITS behind the "Crossroads Cinemas" theater on the "right"{?} and also under "manhole" covers within and outside of the mall] are reportedly ancient tunnels that were discovered by early construction workers and excavators, some of which have been refurbished. Also hints of a human/alien collaboration in the area. The tunnels, catacombs and cavern systems below reportedly involve the following:

Dangerous encounters with reptilian humanoids, federal agency involvement, men seen in a 300 ft. long chamber wearing suits and carrying Uzi machine guns, holographically concealed side passages, a greenish glow seen emanating from behind a locked[?] door in the 3rd sub-level below Crossroads, ancient wooden doors blocking passages that lead north - also on the 3rd sub-level, tunnels under the NE corner of the Crossroads plaza leading south and east that are blocked by metal gates, a huge passage "large enough to drive a semi through" leading south and strung with lights at the bottom of a multi-leveled concrete shaft with descending trap doors, three-toed footprints and a seemingly bottomless pit seen in the cavern from which the "semi" tunnel extends southward, rumors of over 100 miles of passages some ancient and some modern, several accounts of people who have disappeared in the underground labyrinth, paranormal manifestations, and whispered rumors of connections to a vast system of cavern-networks covering an area of about 1000 miles diameter and part of an uncollapsed segment of an ancient global aquifer which collapsed forming the

---

[164] ORION TECHNOLOGY, MIND CONTROL, AND OTHER SECRET PROJECTS, by Val Valerian

ocean beds - a vast system of caverns with penetrates Utah and extends into parts of Idaho, Nevada, Arizona and Colorado.

ZION CANYON –

Reports of a vast underground drainage system which receives the waters of the Great American desert of Utah, Nevada, Arizona and California, stretching from Zion Canyon, to the Grand Canyon of Arizona, to the Carson Sink of Nevada, and to the Mojave desert of California, through which large subterranean rivers flow[165].

VIRGINIA

BELLS COVE –

Near the small village [ghost town?] of Bell's Cove is Buck Hill Caverns, deep within which explorers reportedly discovered a seemingly bottomless shaft, from which emerged the distinct sound of sobbing, or crying and wiling as of a woman in pain[166].

BLUEMONT –

Mt. Weather, in northern Virginia, is a virtual underground city 46 miles from Washington D.C., a C.O.G. [Continuity Of Government[167]] facility, and the hub of the

---

[165] Letter from Chuck Edwards in THE HIDDEN WORLD, issue A-8 [1962]
[166] "The Phantom of Buck Hill Caves", from CORNET magazine, Oct. 1961
[167] Continuity of government (COG) is the principle of establishing defined procedures that allow a government to continue its essential operations in case of nuclear war or other catastrophic event.

FEMA subterranean network [and its underground facilities which exist beneath several major airport terminals].

The infrastructure of Mt. Weather includes microwave communications systems, a small spring-fed lake, a pair of 250,000 gallon water tanks and several ponds, a sewage treatment plant capable of processing 40,000 gallons per day, a hospital, cafeterias, a diesel powered electrical generating plant, private living quarters and dormitories, closed circuit TV, radio and TV studio, massive super-computing facilities which store personal information on millions of Americans, war game simulators, electric cars, etc. Insiders admit that an entire non-representative appointed "back up government" lives in residence within Mt. Weather, being entirely unaccountable to the citizens of the U.S.A.

There are several C.O.G. facilities within a 300 mile radius of Washington D.C., with Mt. Weather being the central coordinator of this "Federal Arc". At least 96 underground C.O.G. facilities exist in Pennsylvania, Maryland, West Virginia, Virginia, and North Carolina[168].

CULPEPER –

COG was developed by the British government before and during World War II to counter the threat of Luftwaffe bombing during the Battle of Britain. The need for continuity-of-government plans gained new urgency with nuclear proliferation.
Countries during the Cold War and afterwards developed such plans to avoid (or minimize) confusion and disorder in a power vacuum in the aftermath of a nuclear attack.
In the US at least, COG is no longer limited to nuclear emergencies; the Continuity of Operations Plan was activated following the September 11 attacks and has been in effect ever since.
[168] UFO Magazine, Vol.7, No.6; Richard Sauder; see also MOUNT WEATHER

A couple miles east of Culpeper, just off Rt.3 in northern Virginia, is Mt. Pony, beneath which lies a large underground government facility maintained by the Federal Reserve and Treasury Dept. The 140,000 sq. ft. facility is said to be supplied with water, food, a generator, communications equipment, etc. At least 5 billion dollars worth of Federal Reserve notes has been stored under Mt. Pony. The facility also monitors major global and banking activity via a "Fed Wire[169]".

LANGLEY –

At least 7 levels of underground facilities beneath the CIA headquarters at Langley, VA, some of which contain recovered alien hardware.

TAZEWELL - 6 miles SW of Tazewell is "Devils Slide Cave", from which an unusual sounds have been heard to emanate[170].

WARRENTON –

The Warrenton Training Center contains an underground relocation center for an unspecified Federal Agency. The U.S. Army maintains two underground facilities near Warrenton, "Station A" on Rt.802 and "Station B" on Bear Wallow Road, on Viewtree mountain. Some suggest that both stations, only a couple miles apart,

---

[169] UFO Magazine, Vol.7, No.6; Richard Sauder
[170] TECH TROGLODYTE [NSS affiliate newsletter], Vol.12, No.2

may be connected underneath. Large antennae towers and AT&T microwave facilities suggest an electronics communications and computing facility. Security at Station A is reportedly more extreme than at Station B[171].

WASHINGTON D.C. -

The House of the Temple, the Scottish Rite Masonic Headquarters, sits atop the pentagram-like street layout of Washington D.C. and reportedly connects to ancient glazed tunnels built by "Atlanteans" in antediluvian times, and also connections to a massive cavern called "NOD" where the NSA, Sirians, and other alien species collaborate in an agenda of global domination. Several D.C. buildings are reportedly connected by underground tunnels, both ancient and modern[172].

WASHINGTON

ELLENSBERG –

Mel Waters tells of a "bottomless shaft" in the Madistash Ridge near Ellensberg, about 10 feet wide. This shaft has also been nicknamed Hell's Hole. One man claims to have dropped an old refrigerator down the shaft but did not hear it hit. Also reports of military men in the area, and residents who were told not to talk about the subject, also rumors that the U.S. military paid the discoverer a "fortune" to shut up about shaft and "disappear"[173].

---

[171] UFO Magazine, Vol.7, No.6; Richard Sauder
[172] Jon Singer; Richard Toronto; WEIRD AMERICA, by Jim Brandon
[173] STRANGE UNIVERSE, April 22, 1997; Art Bell's DREAMLAND radio program

FORT LEWIS –

Many reports state that the Madigan Military Hospital 50 miles south of Seattle is being used by aliens [reptilian] to process military personnel into an alien agenda. The hospital is very high-tech with at least 3 underground levels that are off limits to both civilian and military personnel. Many claim that most of the workers at this Army hospital are "not human", and a powerful electromagnetic field has been reported within and surrounding the hospital area. The nearby Ft. Lewis has been implicated in certain New World Order predatory activities[174].

TACOMA –

At Tacoma there is a strange hole in the back yard of Jim and Harriet Johnson's home, which "devours" everything thrown into it. Cavers explored the hole and saw 3 cone-shaped stones that they could not explain. The Johnson's built a deck over the hole and planned to sell the house, after former owners related their own experiences. The original owner told of being lowered down the hole only to have his oil lamp sucked out of his hands, while another told of filling the hole with marble and 'all kinds of stuff', but the hole 'erupted' spewing stuff all over. Another filled the hole with old tires, but the hole seemed to consume the tires, which began sinking out of site[175].

YAKIMA –

---

[174] Article by Val Valerian in THE LEADING EDGE magazine
[175] : EVERETT HERALD [Everett Washington], March 17, 1980

An alien base reportedly lies below the Yakima Indian Reservation SE of Tacoma, Washington[176].

WEST VIRGINIA

BRAXTON/WEBSTER COUNTIES –
The area bordered by Newville on the west, Helvetia on the east, Cleveland on the north and Hacker Valley on the south [Braxton & Webster counties] contain many subsurface anomalies according to the late husband of British Canadian Joan Howard, an abductee whose husband did survey work in the area.

He told of strange caverns in the area with strange sounds of voices and machinery emerging from within as if beyond the walls, caves containing strange hieroglyphic writings, a pipe that stands out of the ground FAR from any industrial area which ejects a gas flame upwards, a cavern with a deep chasm near which at least one man vanished [from his sleeping bag at night outside the entrance], and one cavernous labyrinth deep within which one man encountered a woman with no hair who spoke to him in an unknown language, yet being unable to understand him she gave up and disappeared into the depths of the labyrinth[177].

POINT PLEASANT –
7 ft. tall reptilian humanoids with 10 ft.-span wings and glowing red hypnotic eyes were observed by several dozen witnesses near Point Pleasant and surrounding

---

[176] THE HOLLOW HASSLE Newsletter, Vol.2, No.2
[177] THE SPACE - OR SOMETHING - CONNECTION, by Joan Howard

communities in the mid 1960's. One of the most concentrated encounter areas was the so-called TNT area where concrete domes led to several miles of underground tunnels where explosives were stored during WWII. Some young people observed one of the creatures which they chased into one of the "domes" which covered the now "capped" tunnel entrances; however when they entered the dome the creature had vanished.

These creatures were described as being something similar to a cross between a humanoid and a pterodactyl, and have been referred to as the Mothmen, Winged Dracos, Winged Serpents, Gargoyles, or Ciakars. John Keel visited the TNT area personally and discovered one large circular area where an almost PHYSICAL atmosphere of terror gripped him and did not leave until he left the "circle[178]".

WEST VIRGINIA, WHITE SULPHUR SPRINGS –

A large C.O.G. [Continuity Of Government] facility exists beneath the Greenbrier Hotel, containing living quarters to house 800 people, meeting rooms and banks of computers and communications equipment, 250 miles SW of Washington D.C. in the Allegheny mountains. The facility also contains a large dormitory, infirmary, shower facilities, television studio, phone booths, dining areas, and a power plant[179].

Though this list is not a complete list as the majority of these underground facilities around the world are by their very nature secret, it does give a n idea of how

---

[178] THE MOTHMAN PROPHECIES, by John A. Keel
[179] UFO Magazine, Vol.7, No.6; Richard Sauder

extensive the underground facilities might actually be. However, when everything written in this volume is taken into considration, there is no doubt that a very strong case can be made for the iidea that the Human race co-existed on this planet for a very long time with races long considered as myths and legends. Clearly, we have shown evidence of Alien Contact.

INDEX

2

29 Palms Marine Base, 152

A

A HOLLOW MOON, 117
Abbey of Saint-Leger, 89
Abzu. *See* House of Far Waters
Achaemenid Empire, 38
Ada, 201
Aetherius Society, 48
Ai, 64
Akhenaten, 35
Akkadian, 15
Albuquerque, 192
Alexander III. *See* Alexander the Great
alien abduction, 13, 47, 79, 80
Allegheny mountains, 204, 221
Alpine, 208, 211
Amenhotep IV. *See* Akhenaten
Ames Research Center, 108
Anaheim, CA, 153
Anânêl, 19
Angel of Death, 4
Anshar, 17
Anu, 16, 17, 23
Anunnaki, 15, 16, 17, 23
Apollo program, 109
Appalachian Mountains, 178
Arâkîba, 18
Araqiel, 19
Archangel Michael, 12
Archuleta mesa, 193
Ariosto, Lodovico, 122
Aristarchus, 114, 117, 125
Aristotle, 37, 106
Armaros, 19
Armârôs, 19
Arnold, Kenneth, 14
Arthurian Camelot, 64
Asâêl, 19
Ascended Master Teachings, 59
Assyrian, 15, 16, 17, 96
Astounding Woodstock Mystery Hole, 203
Athens, 209
Atlanta, 176
Atlantis, 59, 64
Azazel, 19

B

Baal, 83
Babylonian, 15, 16, 17
Bakersfield, CA, 153
Ball, Rex, 175
Baraqel, 19
Barâqîjâl, 19
Barstow, CA, 154
Batârêl, 19
Battle Creek, 183
Battle of Milvian Bridge, 44
Bechtel, 194
Bell-Burnell, Jocelyn, 98
Bell's Cove, 215
Belva Mine, 178
Bezaliel, 19
Binger, 201
Bjarmaland, 65
Black Knight, 18, 97, 98, 99
Black, Jeremy, 16
Book of Daniel, 17
Book of Enoch, 18, 21
Book of Raziel, 19, 20
Book of Revelation, 12
Books of Enoch, 17
Boston, 18, 182
Boulder Dam, 188
Brown Mountain, 201
Burley, 177
Byzantium. *See* Constaninople

C

C.O.G., 160, 166, 215, 216, 221
Cameron, 183, 200
Camp Hero, 199, 200
Camp Irwin, 154
Cargo Cults, 10
Carthage Missouri, 184
Catalina Island, 145
Cave of the Winding Stair, 160
Charlemagne, 29
Chazaqiel, 19
Chicago, 178
China Lake Naval Weapons Test Center, 158
Church of the SubGenius, 49
City of Akhetaton, 36
Ciudad de los Cesares, 64
Clear Lake, 159
Clement of Alexandria, 41
Columbia, 207
Constantinian shift, 43
Constantinople, 88, 89
Continuity Of Government, 160, 166, 215, 221
Crofton, 181
Crossroads Plaza, 214
Culpeper, 217

D

Dallas, 209
Dânêl, 19
Darius III, 38
Dead Horse Camp, 67
Dead Sea Scrolls, 12
Death Valley, 152, 171, 189
Death Valley Men, 171
Deeps Springs, 156
demons, 12, 13
Denton, 146, 209
Devil's Slide cave, 180
Devils Slide Cave, 217
Diadochi, 38
Dixonville, 205
Dobbins Air Force Base, 176
Dobbs, J.R. "Bob", 50
Douglas, 176
Drake, W. Raymond, 38
Druid Arch area, 212
Dugway, 212
Dulce, 146, 192, 193, 194, 195, 196, 197

E

Edict of Milan, 44
Edwards Air Force Base, 145
Eisenhower, President Dwight D., 107
El Dorado, 64
El Moro National Monument, 197
El Paso, 1, 9, 159, 160, 165, 196, 209, 210
El Paso Mountains, 159
Elijah (Elias) the Tishbite, 83
Ellensberg,, 218
Emigrant Canyon, 171
Emperor Constantine the Great, 43
Enki, 23
Enlil, 17, 23
Enoch, 18, 19, 20, 21, 22, 86
Epic of Creation, 16
Epic of Gilgamesh, 17
Epsilon Böotes, 99
ETIDORHPA, 180
Eureka, 188
Eusebius of Caesarea, 44
Exodus, 40
Ezekiel, 28, 40, 52, 53, 86
Êzêqêêl, 19

F

fallen angels, 10, 11, 12, 13, 14, 18, 19, 22
Fallen Ones, 25
false memory syndrome, 80
fantasy-proneness, 80

Fawcett, Colonel Percy Harrison, 65
FEMA, 170, 177, 181, 182, 183, 209, 213, 216
Fort Huachuca, 149
Fort Meade, 181
FORT POLK, 180
Fort Rock Basin, 203
Fort Worth, 210
Ft. Lewis, 219
Ft. Ritchie, 204

G

Gadreel, 19, 20
Gaffney, 207
Gallatin, 208
Gambrel, Earl, 158
Garavanza District (Los Angeles), 164
Genesis, 21, 24, 86
George AFB/Victorville, 169
Giant Rock, 51, 162, 163
Gomorrah, 64
Grand Canyon city, 147
Great Sand Dunes National Monument, 172
Green, Anthony, 16
Greenbrier Hotel, 221
Grey Butte Airport, 163
Grigori, 21, 22

H

Han Emperor Mingti,, 42
Hatshepsut, 31, 33

'haunted' Refugio mine, 208

H

Haycock, George, 177
Heaven's Gate group, 50

Helendale, 160
Herschel, Sir William, 122, 125
Hill, Betty and Barney, 80, 81
Hodges cave, 180
Hoover Dam, 187
House of the Temple, 218
Hudnall, Ken, 9, 210
Hyksos, 32
hypnotizability, 80

I

I.T.T. Corporation, 191
Igigi, 16, 17
International Raëlian Movement, 54
Interplanetary Parliament, 48
Iram of the Pillars, 64
Irmo, 207
Ishtar Gate "Dragon, 96

J

Jared, 86
Jebel Barkal, 33, 34
Jezebel, 83, 85
Jômjâêl, 19
Jordan, S. A., 147
Jubilees, 19, 20
Judgment Day, 18
June Lake, 161

K

Kansas City, 183
Karnak Temple of Amun, 33
Keel, John, 190, 221
Kennesaw Mountain, 176
Kepler, Johannes, 122
Ki, 17
King Abaziah, 83
King Ahab, 83
King, George, 48, 49
Kirtland [AFB] Munitions Storage Complex, 192

Kiser cave, 209
Kishar, 17
Kitezh, Russia, 64
Kokabiel, 20
Kôkabîêl, 18

L

Lahamu, 17
Lahmu, 17
Langley, 217
Lincoln tunnel, 199
Little Cottonwood Canyon, 212
Little Green Men, 98
Lockheed, 160, 161
Lockwood, Wanda, 153
Lord of light, 22
Los Alamos, 170, 193, 194, 196
Los Alamos Labs, 196
Los Angeles, 154, 164, 165, 168
Los Angeles Public Library, 164
Lost City of Z, 65, 78
Lucian of Samosata, 121, 122
Lucifer, 10
lunar city, 123
Lyonesse, 64

M

MacDonald's, 109
Mack, Prof. John E., 80
Madigan Military Hospital, 219
Madistash Ridge, 218
Mahabharata, 28
MAKEN & HANGER, 193
Malden Island, 63
Manhattan, 198
Manuscript 512, 65, 66, 67, 78
Marduk, 16, 23, 24
Mato Grosso, 65, 67
Mayans, 61
Mayflower mine, 189
Maynard, 182
McAlester, 202
McDonnel-Douglas, 161

Mercer Dictionary of the Bible, 22
Mercury Base Camp, 188
Methuselah, 86
Miami, 175
Mitchell Caverns, 160
Mitchell, Jack, 160
Modoc tribe, 150
Moffett Federal Airfield, 108
Montauk Project, 200
Moon, 99, 101, 102, 103, 104, 105, 106, 108, 111, 117, 121, 128, 130, 133, 200
Mt. Blanca [Massif], 172
Mt. Lassen, 163, 170
Mt. Rainier, 170, 173
Mt. Shasta, 150, 151, 164, 172, 213
Mt. Weather, 215, 216
Muhammed, Elijah, 52

N

NASA, 97, 102, 107, 108, 115, 116, 117, 118, 128, 130
Nation of Islam, 52
National Aeronautics and Space Administration. See NASA
Nazi, 59, 108, 190, 191, 192, 213
Nephilim, 10, 13, 14, 18, 21, 25
Nevada City, 189
Nevada Test Site, 156, 157, 188
New Kinsington, 206
Newark, 190, 191
Newkirk, Robert K., 159
Nibiru, 23, 24
Nicephorus, 88, 89
Ninhursag, 23
Noah, 13, 14, 18, 86
NOD, 218
Northrup, 161

O

Oannes, 11
Oklahoma City, 199, 202

Omega Press, 3
Organ Mts., 196
Otuken, 64

P

Pahrump, 189
Paihute Indians, 151
Paititi, 64
Palmdale, 166, 169
Panamint Mountains, 171
Paramus, 191
Penemue, 20
Pepin the Hosrt, 89
Philip II, 37
Pie Town, 197
Pikeville, 178
Pittsburgh, 204, 206
Planet X. *See* Nibru
Point Pleasant, 220
Portland Oregon, 203
PROFORCE Security, 193
Project Moon-Blink, 116
Prophet Elijah, 82
Prophet Ezekiel, 85
Proscelene, 106
psychodynamics, 80
psychopathology, 80

Q

Quincy, 166, 167

R

Radar Cross Section, 160
Râmêêl, 18
Râmîêl, 18
Raven Rock, 204
Redwood Falls, 183
Reno, 190
Rhodes, John, 147
Riverton, 146, 179
Rodulphus Glaber, 89
Rome National Air Base, 200

Rosenberg, Samuel, 29

S

Salem, 180, 213
Salt Lake City Airport, 213
Salton Sea, 167
Samadhi, 49
Samsâpêêl, 19
Samyaza, 18, 20
San Cristobal, 197
San Diego, 167
San Francisco, 51, 108, 159, 167
San Luis Lakes, 172
Santa Rosa, 166, 170
Sariel, 20
Sariêl, 19
Satan, 12, 14
Satarêl, 19
Scientology, 47, 55, 56
Seattle, 219
Sedona, 148
Sêmîazâz, 18
Seven Cities of Gold, 64
Shambhala, 64
Shamsiel, 20
Shaver Mystery, 174, 209
Shaver, Richard S., 173
Shcherbakov, Alexander, 105
Sheaffer, Robert, 80
Shipton, Pennsylvania, 179
Sitchin, Zacharia, 10, 15, 23
sleep paralysis, 13, 80
Sodom, 64
Sofia News Agency, 92
Spaceship Moon Theory, 104
Stoven's Cave, 180
Sumerians, 11, 111
Superstition Mts, 148

T

Tacoma, 173, 219, 220
Tâmîêl, 18
Taos, 146, 197

Tazewell, 180, 217
Tazewell County, 180
Tehachapi Mountains, 168
Tesla, Nikola, 97
Texas
 El Paso, 3, 4
Texas Instruments plant, 209
Thanuny, 32
The Case of the Missing Elephant, 94

'The Man in the Moon', 122

T

Thistle, 213
Thomasville, 177
Three Rivers Pertoglyph site, 95
Three Rivers, New Mexico, 95
Thurmont, 205
Thutmosis III, 29, 31, 34, 35
Tiamat, 17, 111
Trident Engineering Associates, 116
Triumph of the Church, 43
Troy, 63, 65
Truck Coal Mine, 178
Truth or Consequences, 198
Tulli Papyrus, 29
Tulli. Professor Alberto, 29
Tûrêl, 19

U

U.S. Air Force's 21st Space Operations Squadron, 109
UFOs in History, 29
Unarius Academy of Science, 56

underground Pentagon, 176, 204
Universal Industrial Church of the New World Comforter, 51, 52
Universe people, 57
University of Utah, 213
Uriel, 18, 19, 20
Urkunden IV, 32

V

Vandenberg Air Force Base, 145
Vasin, Michael, 104
Vatican Egyptian Museum, 29
Vilcabamba, 63
Vineta, 64

W

Wang. Connie, 4
Warrenton Training Center, 217
Wars of Gods and Men, 27
watchers, 17
Willoughby, Cossette, 166, 167, 198
Wilson, Don, 106, 113

Y

Yakima Indian Reservation, 220
Yeqon, 20
Ys, 64
Yucca Mountain, 170
Yucca Valley, 162

Z

Zaqîêl, 19
Zion Canyon, 215
Zohar, 19, 20

www.ingramcontent.com/pod-product-compliance
Lightning Source LLC
Chambersburg PA
CBHW052022070526
44584CB00016B/1863